THE SECRET OF THE ATOMIC AGE

The present volume is one of a sequence of books by the same author on the application of the Ancient Wisdom to modern living.

The author would be glad to hear from readers who are interested in the subject of human evolution and world progress. Letters may be sent to British Monomark/VSA, London W.C.1, or direct to the publisher who will forward them on to Miss Alder unopened.

VERA STANLEY ALDER

The Secret of the Atomic Age

*A search for Man's
true destiny*

SAMUEL WEISER
New York
1974

First Published 1958
This United States edition 1972
Reprinted 1974

© Vera Stanley Alder 1958, 1972

SAMUEL WEISER, INC.
734 Broadway
New York, N. Y. 10003

ISBN 0-87728-189-4

Contents

Preface

The sequence of books, of which this is the sixth, led up to the challenge of world regeneration which faces us all today. In *When Humanity comes of Age* we looked at the outer possibilities and practical results of right *Being*. We made a blue-print of a much more ideal world civilisation.

This was a study of possible *effects*—effects which would materialise only from the right *causes*.

Those causes still remain a secret—the great secret of the Atomic Age which we will endeavour to uncover in this book.

Man is behaving like a mad genius because there is a gap in his understanding. Genius without morality produces a dangerous chaos, enclosed in the vicious circle of self-centredness from which escape is only possible through complete surrender, and a completely new beginning—in which man finally faces the gap in his understanding—the hiatus between himself and his true destiny.

The Creator is not less than His creations. God, by whatever name we call Him, is therefore the greatest lover, the greatest worker, the greatest artist, and the greatest scientist of all.

Man, called the 'Son of God', is a God in the making with an inconceivable future. He has demonstrated astonishing powers, expressing love, labour, art—and now, science. He has worked through from physical achievement to emotional expression. From there he has passed to the period of mental achievement, the age of science, the gradual approach to the forces of the life behind the form.

The son is approaching closer and closer to the Father. The embryonic God is growing.

But this enthralling development, is, alas, one-sided.

Man's intellect develops but his character remains primitive.

The intellect is only a *tool*, used for good or evil. It is not the man! This tool, the intellect, is not the end of the ladder of progress, but only *half-way there*. And I *mean* half-way!

Man does not yet even realise what he is. 'A Son of God' is a meaningless phrase to him. He looks at his own incredible achievements, his computers, his visits to the moon, and he *does not see* what he is looking at. He does not realise that a creator *must* contain and be capable of all his creations, and even exceed them. He who manipulates atomic energy outwardly, will also be capable of doing it inwardly. He who produces the telephone and the radio will also be capable of communicating by radiation.

By gradually conquering his world from the outer inwards, man has so far left out the innermost—the *cause*! Therefore his world is still causeless, purposeless, dangerous.

He cannot face up to his Father God—Who has produced certain laws—to fulfil a certain Purpose, the Purpose of evolution on this planet. He has been given throughout history teaching about these Laws and the ways in which he must develop his Godhood. But he is learning the hard way. He still is an utterly sleeping Godlet! He lives focused in his lower brain, embedded in physical consciousness, whilst the living forces of life are pressing in upon him and the radiations of reality are expanding within him. Either he must *give* himself to reality—to the Laws of his Creator—or he will explode and burn up.

That this is already beginning to happen is proved by the enormous percentage of the community now in mental care—and by the chaotic and dangerous situation of humanity in total.

In spite of science, man no more knows what the world is really like than does a dragonfly still imprisoned in its hard chrysalis beneath the dark water.

What does the human being know about his own atomic energy and how to release it? What does he know about his own radio-activity and process of transmutation? What does he know about the future of himself and his potentials, and his future companionships when he will have broken out of his present hard and impenetrable mental chrysalis? What lies ahead when he has earned his freedom—and how shall he begin to do so?

When man becomes his own computer, his own space traveller, his own television and telephone— when he achieves his own 'dialogue' with the rest of nature—shares in the wielding of the Laws of life itself—then he will become his own co-operator with the Divine Purpose within himself.

Those Great Ones who have achieved a measure of Their Godhood already, have stood by infant humanity always, and are standing now, awaiting the time when men finally turn to Them in surrender and dedication to that which They represent and, which is the sole gateway to freedom, to growth, and to joy unimaginable. That which They represent, that which is still the gap in man's understanding can be expressed in one word.

That word is—INTEGRITY.

The quality of complete Integrity is illimitable. It leads from realisation to realisation, from responsibility to responsibility, from change to change.

It brings about man's transmutation.

The Ten Commandments are based on Integrity. They are evaded by all 'Christian' countries today.

That is the gap which must be filled before men can reap their real atomic heritage.

V.S.A.

London 1972

Introduction

Scientists have succeeded, with incredible brilliance, in analysing the atom, and delving into its even smaller component particles.

They have come to know a great deal about it. They have achieved the fantastic task of splitting it and of setting free the mysterious energy which, as they had suspected was locked within it.

They have proved that the atom is a most complex organism.

At the same time they have proved that it is composed of nothing but positive and negative electricity. They have somehow been able to reconcile these two wildly contradictory statements.

They have discovered how to disarrange the adjustments within the atom in order to change one element into another, something which would have been considered an impossible miracle a very few years ago. They have ascertained that in the normal evolutionary processes of nature, such changes take place, although at an infinitely slower pace.

The scientists are going to do wonderful things with these discoveries. Possibly the days of the Atom Bomb will pass away like a nightmare, and mankind will be invited to reap all the benefits which could acrue from the peaceful uses of atomic energy. Perhaps his hours of labour will be halved, and his problems of lighting, heating and industrial energy improved and cheapened beyond his wildest dreams.

Where, however, will man himself stand in face of this new atomic epoch? What will it do to you and to me? How will it affect our health, our way of living, our understanding of our *joie de vivre*? The impact of a new discovery can work equally for good or bad for the individual. The industrial age has already shown us this. Are we going to have a personal relationship with man's new servant, the atom, or are we going to leave it all to the scientists?

Let us not forget that we ourselves are composed of atoms. There are vast hidden reserves of power within every one of us, within each atom of each molecule of each cell in our bodies. Each atom and each cell is an entity built upon a pole of positive and negative electricity. Man, the aggregate of his cells, is built in that way also.

For untold centuries the savants or scientists have been aware of the great mysteries locked within all living things, those mysteries and laws which have produced sentient creatures out of nothing but energy of differing vibrational rates. They believed that an almighty Intelligence was at work behind it all. They declared that man himself was potentially a finite replica of this all-pervading Intelligence, and that as such he should be able to learn to play his part and fulfil his own mysterious destiny within the whole Scheme.

They tried to do this in two ways. The first method was to study how to wield and control the hidden forces of man's own complex nature. This science was known by many names in many climes, but perhaps it is best known to us as the science of Yoga. This can briefly be described as the practice of uniting man's separate parts —the physical body, the mind, the heart and the soul—

so that they can become perfect instruments for the expression of Divine Purpose. In most people these parts are insulated one from another, or at cross purposes, producing a chaotic personality, and thus a chaotic collective community—a chaotic world economy.

The second method involved a study of the way in which life was built up in the smallest organic entity, the mineral atom, and of the long evolutionary process through which it passed until its ultimate essence was released.

The savants of old blended both esoteric and material knowledge in the production of a science which was intended to speed up the processes of nature, transmute the minerals and capture the essences and the elixirs locked within them. With these powerful substances they claimed to produce rapid transmutation in both man and metal, developing in the former rejuvenation and regeneration, and in the latter—gold!

This age-old science is known to us as Alchemy. It was the predecessor and parent of medicine and chemistry. It was concerned, moreover, with atomic energy and its release.

Alchemy worked, however, in alignment with the laws laid down by nature, and tried to speed up natural processes. It did not work through the use of violence and of explosive activities, as does modern science. Thus it did not produce violently dangerous radiations, and deadly poisonous by-products.

Charlatans existed in Alchemical circles, just as they exist in every other sphere of study. But the science itself was a profound and revered one. It was, at its best, an expression of man's understanding of and co-operation with the Divine Intelligence, or 'God'. Through an understanding of the transmutation which takes place in minerals, man is able to appreciate the same process latent within himself. Through speeding up that process in the mineral, and refining it to its ultimate powerful inner essence, man realises that if he will submit the constituents of his own being to the same purifying process he will refine away all grossness both material and invisible, and release his own essence or spiritual power. It is the same process throughout. The electrical forces existing in both matter and mind can be used to burn away dross, to alter vibrational rates, and to produce complete changes of elemental substances, and of quality, in both the mineral atom and the cells which it builds in the body of man.

The mind of man is an electrical instrument, given to him to be used in this transmuting process. The most subtle of all forms of Alchemy is the transmutation of knowledge into wisdom. The materially minded person will not even know the difference between the two. Knowledge is the accumulation of facts. These facts, or elements, are static of themselves, but the processes of the mind manipulate and transmute them until a quite new product is born. We call it an 'idea'. If this product is produced by a mind in alignment with the laws of nature (God), it will be an expression of *Wisdom*, which is the elixir, distillation or essence of the genius within man. If, on the other hand, it is produced by a mind focused in self-interest and materialism, it will have a destructive and explosive quality. This is because wisdom always works towards unification and interplay, in line with natural law; it shares, and radiates and gives out. Whereas a self-centred mind accumulates, draws unto itself, rather than radiates, creating a self-protecting shell and short-circuits the subtle and electrical interchange of evolutionary living.

When the grossness of selfishness in human beings has been transmuted and burnt away, all of his cells become radioactive. Their radiations have a luminosity and colour which is observable by certain people who have extra-developed sight, and has been represented for thousands of years all over the world as a nimbus or halo. The halo of the saint could perhaps be analysed and explained as a scientific fact by those experts of today who are engaged in the photography and measurement of radiations.

A person who has become radioactive, or who is able to transmute the atoms in his own body through the electrical forces of the mind, is as omnipotent compared with the undeveloped human being as nuclear energy is compared with the energy emitted by burning coal or wood. Such a person could have access to, and control of, an unlimited flow of power from within his own periphery. He could use it for a variety of purposes: for rejuvenation; for the acceleration of mental powers; for the withstanding of heat and cold; or for the radiation of powerful thoughts for the help of mankind.

The atomic energy which man is learning to release through science is actually the *vehicle* of spirit, the nearest substance to spirit. It is that which the spiritual impulse, which impels life and growth, uses in the creation of matter. It creates matter through the manipulation and control of *differing rates of vibration*, nothing more.

Man has now learnt how to change one element into another through stimulating this inner energy into premature action. It is awe-inspiring and dangerous work.

In Yoga and other ancient sciences of self-development, the electrical fires of the mind were used to initiate a similar process in order to release the energy of the bodily atoms. This produced what was called the Kundalini Fire, which was equally dangerous unless under the control of an utterly selfless mind. In a selfish personality it of course produced an explosive situation, in which the brain cells were sometimes burnt up and insanity was the unfortunate result.

Humanity is now faced with most dangerous but wonderful possibilities. Through its own efforts it has reached a degree of *knowledge* which could bring omnipotence and fulfilment in personal and world affairs—provided that this knowledge can be allied to wisdom (or the realisation of Divine Will and Plan).

If this is not achieved, disaster faces us all.

The challenge can no longer be avoided. It is pressing urgently upon the entire world today. That is why compromise at present could be even more disastrous than evil-doing, for it delays progress, whereas evil-doing burns itself out.

How wonderful if we could rise to this historic occasion, the inauguration of the Atomic Age, and learn to play our rightful part in it through a full understanding of its significance, and thus reap our glorious heritage. Whilst it is being worked out in its material aspect by modern science, let us keep the balance by studying and developing its fundamental basic aspect within ourselves. Thus we may take our places in the vanguard of progress as the exponents of that Wisdom without which humanity will never win through.

In order to do this we propose to embark on a fascinating exploration. The mind of man is such that when once he has allowed it fully to grasp a situation (that is to say, without prejudice) subconscious action is always taken in accordance with that situation. That is why it has been said that 'sin' is really ignorance—ignorance of the laws of life or of the full facts of any situation. Therefore, if we can once fully understand the situation in regard to the atomic energy within ourselves, we will automatically begin to gain control of it, especially if we can understand its true relationship to the atomic energy of modern science.

We will therefore explore these secrets of life in their several spheres and phases. Firstly, we will study the atom itself, its creation, development and fulfilment. Secondly, we will study it as it exists in the human body, and explore its relationship to ourselves. Thirdly, we will summarise the science of the old Alchemists and find out, as nearly as we can, just what they were trying to do. We will then compare this with what modern science is achieving.

Finally, we will consider what both the modern physical sciences and the modern metaphysical sciences are demonstrating today. It is possible that such an exploration may make more clear to us man's position in the Divine Scheme, and that we will have grasped the situation sufficiently to undergo a mental transmutation so that our lives will be irresistibly oriented to the new values, new practices and new powers inherent in the Atomic Age. If we are sincere enough, we may become the channels for that Wisdom which is so desperately needed at the present time.

Christ stated explicitly that He would 'Return'. In fact He said that He would always be with us—possibly in that realm of vibrations from which materialism has been insulating us for so long. Science is opening up the way for us in an almost terrifying approach to the spiritual sphere itself. Can it not be that if we will grasp the new knowledge and the proffered opportunity in the right way, a most marvellous realisation and experience awaits us?—an experience, moreover, which we should be sharing with those fellow-spirits all over the world who also await 'Him' under whatever name they know

Him, God's Messenger, the Ever-Coming One (as the ancient Egyptians called Him) Who appears throughout world history at cyclic intervals, to save and to lead mankind.

PART ONE

I

The beginnings of creation

THE question which has tantalised men throughout history is that of the origin of life. This ultimate mystery will doubtless remain locked to our finite minds, at any rate for aeons to come. However, much is known, and much more has recently been discovered, of those forces which cause the atom to take shape, and of the substances which form it.

In Genesis it is stated that God created the world in two ways: by His Will or Intention, and with His spoken Word.

The uttered word produces vibration, each syllable, vowel and consonant creating a different vibration. Such a vibration at once produces a little vortex or vacuum in the ether, around which the ether begins rapidly to circulate in an effort to refill it. Thus a tiny centre of activity is set up, because this vortex, being of a definite shape, becomes the recipient of a corresponding ray and electrical charge. For, as we know, 'nature abhors a vacuum', and into it the life force rushes to create an entity. A polarity is formed, that is to say a core of electricity both positive and negative, a tiny replica of the magnetic pole which runs through our planet and every creature living upon it, and which is also itself a replica of the pole which holds our solar system together.

It is recognised that the atom bears a strong resemblance to a solar system, having a positive and fiery nucleus or core, representing the sun. This nucleus is magnetic, holding to itself everything within the radius of its influence, its ring-pass-not or aura. This aura is built in layers something like an onion. Each layer can provide the orbit in which a 'planet' swings around the central sun. We know these planets or satellites as electrons. They are negative to their sun, and held to it by the attraction which the stronger body and higher vibration have for the lesser.

In considering the character of the atom we must be careful to remember that the scientist of today is still only dealing with the grosser physical atom which is precipitated upon our planet, and from which 'solid matter' is formed. We shall have to consider the idea that within the infinitely small orbit of the scientist's atom are packed millions of much smaller and finer atoms, and that these are the real atoms which produce all organised and living forms. Later on we will give examples to prove the existence of these finer atoms, and that they travel through space on the cosmic waves. They are so subtle that it could almost be said that they *are* the cosmic waves. Nevertheless they people the atmosphere with untold millions of mineral particles, so fine and of so high a vibration that they pass through 'solid' matter very easily and invest it with their life and qualities. They are the radioactivity of suns and planets outside the radius of our solar system.

We know that our earth, the 'fallen planet', was first in a gaseous state and then cooled and solidified. Many of the mineral substances which then took shape became very solid and heavy indeed, their atoms becoming unrecognisable from their kinsmen, the particles of the cosmic rays. For a volatile and pulsing atom to be thus imprisoned in heavy crystals of comparatively static matter is no pleasure. It is surely a severe discipline. We can imagine that all the atom longs for is movement, lightness and freedom once more. Anything which stimulates the atom will increase this natural desire.

Man, the human being, has also suffered and shared the same fate as the atom. Himself an immortal spark of genius, subtle and high-powered as the cosmic rays, he is compressed into a prison of 'solid matter', a fleshly form, wherein he has forgotten his identity and his god-like powers. He has had to work out a long history of discipline, until he shall learn how to raise himself and at the same time the atoms who share his fate and destiny, out of their imprisonment into a free and conscious spiritual existence once again.

This transformation of man and atom, and of all life upon this planet, is accomplished by a process which we know as transmutation. By this we mean the transmuting of lower and slower vibrations into higher and faster ones, the changing of that which is heavy and gross into that which is ethereal and subtle, and more powerful.

Transmutation is the universal way of evolution and regeneration of all life upon this planet. It takes place within the atoms, the elements, the cells and man himself. The fascinating fact is, however, that without the existence of man upon his planet, transmutation would be enormously slowed down and incomplete. For man, in the very act of achieving his own transmutation and liberation, achieves it for the other kingdoms of nature too.

We are not here speaking of scientific experiments and processes, but of the processes of natural evolutionary living.

However, in order to understand this process of trans-mutation, which is nothing less than the return of matter into spirit, of substance into energy, of effects into causes, of impotence into power, of ignorance into wisdom, we must first study very carefully the compo-sition, character and life cycle of the atom. As the atom is composed of energy organised by a state of vibration, we must first consider what vibration is.

Vibration is the pulse which beats in every living entity. It is the very movement of life and of living. It is the language of life also, for the rate at which vibration takes place determines the character and quality of that which vibrates. An atom takes shape around its core of life because that life, by means of its vibration, draws around it the substances it needs, builds them into a certain form, and holds them to itself with great tenacity (or atomic energy).

A vibration is set up when, as we have mentioned, the life force establishes an electrical polarity. For instance, in the creation of an atom, a tiny north and south pole, with its association of positive and negative electricity, takes form. This situation instigates oscillation or vibra-tion, which sets up a magnetic field. The cosmic electri-cal waves are absorbed at the north pole of the atom, energy is stored by the negative aspect of the pole, whilst the positive aspect controls and emits oscilla-tions (vibrations) at the individual rate of the atom in question; and these vibrations propel radiations at wave-lengths of a size and frequency which accords with them. This is the situation which takes place in any living creature, whether it be an atom, a cell, a human being or a planet.

The slower and lower the rate of vibration, the longer are its wave-lengths, and the coarser and heavier is the life expressed thereby. The faster or higher the rate of vibration, the subtler and more powerful is the life expressed, and the shorter and more penetrating are its radiations and wave-lengths. Each type of radiation can be found to have its specific note and colour.

The positive electricity at work within the atom is its male aspect, the aspect of activity, whereas the negative electricity is the female aspect, which is concerned with the storage of energy. The same situation is found within the living cell, within the insect, the animal or the human being. In the latter the pole lies along the spine, with its positive and negative currents. These have always been recognised and had their symbolic names in all great ancient cultures, as for instance the Yin and the Yang of the Chinese, and the Ida and Pingala of India.

It will help us as we go along to bear closely in mind, if possible, a realisation of our great limitations, as human beings, in relation to time and space. To the Almighty Creator there are no such limitations. We can realise that He is able to function, to plan and to design on a scale infinitely smaller than we can even imagine, with the aid of all our scientific instruments. His powers are also in control of forms and spaces too vast for us to conceive.

The ancient scientists, who realised this, gave us the precept 'As above, so below'. This expressed the fact that conditions within an atom or a man can give us the clue to conditions obtaining in a larger body such as a planet, or indeed a solar system.

When an atom is formed it allocates to itself an envelope of ether like that around the earth, a ring-pass-not, held inviolable by its own magnetism. In the atom this globe of ether (within which the solid core of the atom is but the tiniest speck) is organised in layers of successive magnetic intensities. Each of these layers can accommodate up to a definite number of satellites which swing round the central sun. The sun of the atomic solar system, which we call the nucleus, is principally composed of one or more particles of positive electricity, called protons, whereas the satellite is a particle (or unit) of negative electricity and is called an electron.

Since these first elementary theories were put forward about the construction of the atom, much more has been learned. The existence of many other constituents of the atom has been determined, together with the possibilities of many kinds of activity, reaction and change within the atom itself. In fact the atom has been proved to be a most complex organism. The new facts which continue to come to light about it are causing scientists to modify much of what they already believed.

We now know that the smallest particle of that which we call 'matter' is simply a particle of electricity which is able to separate itself off as a tiny individual form and *retain its identity* as distinct from pure formless electrical energy. It is from these tiny sparks that our physical world is made. The manner of this making is truly wonderful in its complex simplicity!

The Creator used the very fires of His mind with which to work. He divided them into two kinds of electricity, known in the past as the male and female aspects of life, and known by today's scientists as positive and negative electrical energy.

The tiniest spark of negative electricity is called an electron. It was so named by the Greeks because they discovered it when applying friction to amber, which they had called 'electra'. The diameter of the electron has been assessed as a million millionth of a centimetre, and its electric charge as ten thousand millionths of an electrostatic unit.

The tiniest spark of positive electricity is called a proton. Its mass is 1846 times smaller than that of the electron. But it exerts a strong magnetic attraction upon the electron, and this is the basis of the formation of the atom.

The first atom to be formed was the hydrogen atom. One proton attracted one electron into its aura. Thus the positive and negative pole was set up, the atom began to spin upon its axis, a magnetic field was formed, as well as a certain rate of vibration and the radiation of a certain wave-length. The electron revolved round in an orbit within the atmosphere held by the power of the proton nucleus. This globe of atmosphere, which surrounds every atomic nucleus, is very large in comparison with the nucleus. In the case of the hydrogen atom, its nucleus occupies only one thousand billionth of the atmospheric volume of the atom. It is therefore very similar in proportion to that of our sun in the atmosphere of its solar system. The electron moves around through the globe of atmosphere at the rate of ten million million million times a second, thus enclosing the globe in its own negative electrical charge or cloud, and forming a complete ring-pass-not which isolates the atom as a separate entity. Like repels like, and the negative exterior of the atom repels the negative exteriors of other atoms who come near it.

The hydrogen atom, with its one proton and one electron, is the simplest of the atoms, and the least heavy. It is the basic brick, as it were, from which all the others are built. It is the unit from which all the others are measured. Its nucleus bears a positive electrical charge of one nuclear unit. It is this charge which determines the nature and character of the atom formed. The atoms of all other elements are determined by the number of positively charged protons in the nucleus. The number of electrons held in the orbit of any atom is the same as the number of protons in its nucleus. The former swing around the nucleus, each patrolling its own stratum in the atomic atmospheric envelope.

At present there are around 100 known elements in nature, from which all compounds and substances are produced. These elements have been arranged in a long sequence, or table, in accordance with their atomic positive charge, which is determined by their having from one to ninety-two protons in their nucleus. The element at the beginning of the list is hydrogen, with one proton and one electron in its atom. The element at the end of the list is uranium, with ninety-two positive protons and ninety-two negative electrons in its atom.

We thus have a wonderful arrangement, which can produce the character and wave-length of all the different elements. It can produce everything except weight, that is to say, it can produce only atoms of rather light weight and volatile character. In order to produce heavy solid matter, the Creator had to devise something further. This He did by taking a proton and an electron and binding them so closely together that the globe of atmosphere was missing, as was also their positive and negative electrical activity. In other words, they were clasped together so tightly that their electrical energy was rendered temporarily neutral, being used in the binding. Scientists have therefore called them 'neutrons'. We can understand that such a neutron, without any atmosphere must be both heavy and 'solid'. So in order to give weight and solidity to an element, one or more of these neutrons are packed tightly amongst the protons in the nucleus. This, of course, is not the whole of the story. Almost every week more varieties of particles with different attributes, are discovered within the amazing atom, but for our purpose this must suffice.

Thus we find that in uranium, the heaviest element, the nucleus contains ninety-two positive protons, and its atmosphere contains ninety-two negative electrons. But the nucleus *also* contains one hundred and forty-six neutrons. It is this tremendously compressed and imprisoned energy which brings about natural radioactivity as found in many minerals. Stimulation by heat, pressure, radiations and other phenomena, will raise the vitality of the nucleus, until the inner expansions produces an explosion. A particle or particles are shot out from the nucleus together with rays of released energy. This is radioactivity.

Some of these rays are known as the beta and gamma rays. The uranium nucleus, having lost one positive charge, has *changed to that of another element*, and the atom belongs now to a different place in the table of elements! This process can be repeated until our atom has changed its character five or six times, gradually becoming less and less radioactive, until it may finish up as radium-lead, plus, of course, the more ethereal elements and compounds which the escaping particles have formed elsewhere.

This is the process of transmutation, as it takes place in the mineral world. It is the return of the Prodigal Son of the mineral kingdom back to its more subtle place in the Divine Breath. It has escaped from the imprisonment of solid matter. It has developed the will and the energy to obtain its freedom and emancipation back into the spheres of cosmic radiation and of Divine Intelligence. It has achieved its evolution.

This same process of transmutation is taking place in all the other kingdoms in nature, although less easily

discernible to the modern scientist. He does not yet
know that his tiny atom of the laboratory is really a
monster, packed with innumerable smaller 'cosmic'
atoms, who are the basic vital activators of the whole
scheme. It is quite easy to prove the existence of these
very fine atoms by means of some simple experiments,
but we will mention these later on.

The electrons in the *outer* shell of an atom's atmosphere can be detached or shot off in a number of ways.
Scientists have perhaps not yet realised that when once
a negative electron has been detached from its parent
atom, and is travelling through the air, it at once
becomes positive. It *must* do, or it would disintegrate, so
it therefore *positively* holds together all the cosmic particles which compose it as an entity. *But* when it comes
in contact with a large atom of greater positivity than
itself, which seeks to appropriate it, it may at once give
allegiance, become negative to the greater body, accept
the vacant place in its orbit, and take up its patrolling
duties once more. This is in accordance with one of
nature's fascinating laws, already mentioned: that of
the magnetism which a larger body of a stronger or
higher vibration exerts over a smaller body.

This means that every entity in nature is positive to
all the lesser atoms and cells and radiations within its
being, and negative to any higher or more powerful
radiation outside of itself. It is necessary to bear this
law carefully in mind, as it is basic to the subject of
our research. That great atom, our planet, is positive
to and draws unto itself, everything within its magnetic
field, including its satellite (or electron!), our moon.
This magnetism creates what we know as the law of
gravity.

Our planet, in its turn, is negative to a greater body,
the sun, and acts as an electron to it, helping to create

its negative electrical ring-pass-not, in company with the other planets of our solar system. Our sun, with its satellites, is itself negative to and acts as an electron to a still larger sun. This theme, although so far undiscovered by modern science, has always been taught by the 'Ageless Wisdom'. We may conclude that shooting stars are particles which are shot out from a nucleus or solar body during its radioactive transmutations.

This same process of transmutation can be traced in all the kingdoms of nature. It is already known that certain insects, trees and fruits are radioactive. As for man himself, his place in the processes of transmutation is really the goal of our research. In the mineral world it is the heaviest and most solid of metals and minerals which contain the greatest quantity of compressed life force. Our Creator made every living creature by using the mineral world as His building material. He anchored His own life to the earth within its most earthbound and tightly imprisoning forms: the mineral rocks. Such terrible pressure upon imprisoned spirit produced many things of beauty, which we know as jewels. They are the highest creative expression of the mineral world.

Whilst the modern scientist has continued with his really wonderful efforts to decipher and to use that which he can neither see nor touch, he has discovered more and more complexities and activities within the atom. Finally, he has learnt how to produce the transmutation of one element into another. He has discovered one by one the secrets of the inner life and power of the atom. By his patience and daring he is penetrating to the very feet of the Creator. In the end he may be able to say:

'Almighty, I now almost know how You made our world!'

He is achieving this amazing result by working from the outside inwards, by concerning himself only with what he calls 'scientific facts' and deductions. He leaves entirely alone the enormous volume of writings and teachings on the subject of the formation and purpose of the universe, which we have inherited from the intelligentsia of earlier civilisations. He has a 'scientific' mind, by which he means that he wishes to have objective proof of everything in which he agrees to believe with his concrete or materialistic brain.

It is courageous thus to work from 'scratch', without help or suggestion from all the great minds that have gone before. The result will be that when eventually the modern scientist reaches, by his own methods, almost to the throne of God, and exposes or 'proves' the laws and arrangements by means of which the Divine Purpose is working out amongst men, he will have opened the doors of spiritual truth to the many intellectuals and mind-ruled people in the world today. He will have performed a great service to humanity.

This is because the general public is at present in the stage of developing its intellect. A large number of people want to think things out for themselves. They can no longer accept the many 'unproven' statements in the teachings offered to them, especially in the religious sphere. If they are to accept spiritual truths and laws, they wish to absorb them consciously and with at least partial understanding, instead of blindly and on trust as hitherto. They have a growing wish really to know, not to be misled or moulded into a pattern to suit authority. This would appear to be the beginning of a true adulthood in humanity, the taking of responsibility for personal development and action.

It seems likely that quite soon the work of the modern scientist will bring proof of the truth of certain of the spiritual teachings which are our heritage from the past. Then, the precocious mentality once satisfied, men will be able to accept and live by the Divine Laws of the universe, and the world's problems will be resolved by natural means.

C

2

The riddle of the ether

THE mystery that haunts the laboratories of today like a tantalising ghost that will not be exorcised, and which is neither there nor not there, is that of the ether! To be or not to be is certainly the burning question in this case.

Throughout history much has been taught about that vast ocean of invisible 'space' in which solid objects such as our earth find themselves suspended without visible means of support. Our scientist firmly turns his back on 'ancient superstitions' and continues on his search for that 'ether which may or may not be', without a clue!

Even such a genius as Einstein 'decided that most known phenomena could be better explained if the ether was ignored', as Dorothy Fisk says, in *Modern Alchemy*. This is certainly a most unfortunate position to put us in, if the ether really exists.

If we are to think the question out quite quietly for ourselves it seems fairly easy to decide that so-called space must be a very crowded substance indeed.

For instance, there are thousands of archetypal forms in nature, which have been designed and 'fixed' in the atmosphere by some mighty Intelligence. Some of the simpler types are those of the crystals. When physical substance takes form, its atoms congeal, solidify or crystallise around certain lines of force which play throughout space, producing invisible forms in their myriads. A snow crystal can form itself instantly when a given condition of temperature and pressure is present. But how does it take its perfect and often complicated, and always true, shape? Obviously that form must be in the atmosphere, as it can be nowhere else. There must be some stratum of the atmosphere which is holding forms, forms everywhere, radiating in every direction.

If minute droplets of water freeze in mid air, turning into snowflakes, they produce exquisite crystals of many complex forms. In what mould were these forms cast? How was their perfect symmetry controlled?

If these same droplets had not congealed until they reached a window-pane, they would have taken on other forms as they froze and crystallised—those of the plant world, as we know from the beautiful fern shapes which we find on frosty roads or windows. Even the type of plant form produced would depend on how much sunshine was reaching it at the time of freezing.

These extraordinary facts in nature, and many others, prove to us that the invisible (to us) atmosphere contains a network of radiant forms or moulds, to which grosser matter clings as it congeals. This network of forms is an independent substance or framework, quite apart from the millions of atoms and their particles which are radiating in every direction.*

Furthermore, it would appear that, *in the same space,* different archetypal forms can exist, interpenetrating but independent of each other, and that matter will crystallise around one or the other according to the degree of light and temperature which is present at the time. We are therefore faced with a complex situation in the space around us which challenges all our powers of comprehension. We must also recognise that these

* See *The Fifth Dimension*

creative archetypal lines of force are of such a nature that they must be passing through our own beings all the time, creating crystallisations of one type or another according to the conditions which our bodies offer to them.

If our optic nerves were not so severely limited to a range of very few vibrations, we would be able to see much of this invisible activity. If our senses of touch were more finely developed we would be able to feel it. As it is, we remain blind to and unaware of that ocean of life which is feeding us and building us from moment to moment, and in the midst of which we are *comparatively* dead and inert, so enclosed are we in the grosser and 'louder' vibrations of more solid matter.

This mysterious substance which spreads through space has been loosely termed 'the ether' for many generations. The growing accuracy of present-day scientists, however, is defied by the fact that a whole series of contradictory attributes are at work in this 'ether'. Therefore they are unable to give it a coherent character and activity. As we remarked, they have not, at the present time, the clue! They do not know whether to think of it as composed of matter, of energy or of something different from either.

In approaching this problem one of our questions must be, what is the smallest size at which a physical atom can exist? In other words, how tenuous can matter become and still remain matter? We have already mentioned that the atom of the laboratory is in reality quite a gross entity, packed with thousands of finer atoms which are the real instigators of the activities of living. Perhaps we can digress for a moment and suggest ways in which this statement can be borne out.

Most of us have heard of Colour Therapy. This is an interesting science which deals with the effect of colours

used in healing, with their place in psychology, and with
the fact that they represent the expression, quality and
attributes of the various minerals. Yellow, for instance,
is associated with sulphur, which as we know has
stimulating and purgative qualities. If we take a closed
yellow glass vessel filled with pure water, and expose it
to the sunshine for some hours, there is an interesting
result. The combination of sun's rays and water (the
latter being a great absorber), together with the vibration of the yellow colour, will attract the fine cosmic
atoms of sulphur from the atmosphere, and they will
pass through the glass into the water. The latter will
soon possess a high sulphur content, although in a very
subtilised form. Taken as a medicine it will have the
results associated with sulphur. Also, as sulphur produces combustion and putrefaction, the water in the
yellow vessel will soon become foul.

On the other hand, if pure water be exposed to sunshine in a sealed blue glass vessel it will attract atoms of
mineral such as cobalt, having an antiseptic and seda-
tive quality, which is effective when used medicinally.
The water in such a blue glass vessel will keep indefi-
nitely.

Each of the other colours of the spectrum is associated
with certain minerals and with the qualities and
activities of such minerals. This interesting therapy will
give us proof that mineral atoms fine enough to pass
through glass are readily obtainable from the air.

Another way of proving our point would be by
studying the Bach system of healing by flowers. The
blossoms of the flowers are soaked in clear water in the
sunshine, and once again the combination of sun and
water draws out the finest essence of the flower, composed of course of very fine atoms, into the water. It is
then bottled. But the medicine is made by taking only

one drop of liquid from the bottle and mixing it with a quantity of plain water, thus giving a triturated or homeopathic dose. In Homeopathy, or the science of the infinitely small dose, the atoms of curative substance are thinned out by such means until they are quite untraceable, and yet their effects in disease are far more powerful than those of the cruder drugs. This is because the finer cosmic atoms have been set free and given scope, and they have power to pass through the most delicate tissues straight to the source of need within the human body.

In fact such atoms can travel at speeds almost incredible to us, passing right through the bodies of the grosser atoms. The ordinary electron, say of the hydrogen atom, has been reckoned to revolve round the nucleus ten million million million times a second, spinning as it goes! As for the neutron, scientists estimate that when it escapes from the atom its velocity reaches 20,000 miles per second. We can see that a sufficiently fine cosmic atom might be able to travel almost at the speed of 'electricity'. If this is so, then a very fine atom could dash round the world in a few moments. If I breathed out such an atom in England it could be breathed in by someone in Australia before I had finished taking a second breath! This, of course, would not be the case with the atoms which the scientist is studying. The speed of their voyage through the air is interrupted, in the average way, by constant collisions with other atoms or particles. The flying atoms are also slowed down by the impact of their own magnetised sphere of atmosphere with the outer air. The case of the neutron, however, is different. Having practically no atmospheric globe of its own, and being consequently minute in mass, it can shoot through the atmospheric globes of other atoms without pressure upon them or itself. The neutron has been reckoned to travel three miles without slowing down to any appreciable extent. If this can be done by one of the most solid and heavy of particles, we can begin to see the possibilities of speed and distance available to the minute cosmic atoms. They could almost be 'everywhere at once'.

A study of Homeopathy would show us that it is based on the fact that the division of the atoms into their tiniest units, or 'cosmic' atoms, has no apparent limit, and that such untraceable atoms are very potent in their action.

If, therefore, there is no limit to the smallness of an atom, could it not be that the substance we call 'ether' is formed of a yet finer type of atom than the mineral one? We have observed that the Creator formed the mineral atom by combining a positive electrical spark with a much larger negative electrical spark. Is it not possible that He devised a slightly different combination in order to form another type of matter, which we call ether, to act as intermediary between the more solid 'inert' matter and the life forces which seek to feed and build it?

If we turn to the Ageless Wisdom, we will find, in fact, that this is said to be the case. The ether is stated to be a finer form of physical matter, an ocean of fine atoms in which all visible life floats, and with which it is permeated, and by means of which all the electrical life forces pass into the more solid and crystallised forms.

Furthermore, the atoms of the ether were said to exist in four sizes, forming four separate grades or types of ether. Each of these ethers was said to have a different character and function. The coarsest or lowest grade was named the 'Chemical Ether' according to one ancient system. It was said to be the vehicle for those energies which produce growth and maintenance of the physical forms. Then comes a finer ether named the Life Ether, along which play the forces which induce propagation of the species. Thirdly, there is the Light Ether along which travel the powers inherent in light, and which produce chlorophyl in plants, colour in nature, and the development of the five senses. The fourth and finest ether is called the Reflecting Ether. Its inconceivably tiny atoms are said to be photographic and to store records of all that has taken place. They provide the mystery called memory, and are the medium through which thoughts make impressions on the brain.

The Ageless Wisdom, together with its many modern interpreters and amplifiers,* gives lengthy teachings on the activities of the 'four ethers'. To the modern scientist such writings are either completely unknown or completely taboo. He feels it to be his duty to 'prove' everything as he goes along. He is not yet convinced that ether exists, because of its contradictory qualities. If he could conceive of four separate although interpenetrating ethers, each with different activities, he might begin to feel his way towards a means of discovering them. For, without the ethers, we have no explanation of how any of the activities in nature can take place.

Solids, liquids and gases each possess quite different properties. They are able to interpenetrate each other without losing their individual characters. (Imagine, for instance, a sponge in a bowl of water through which smoke has been blown.) Can we not therefore conceive of other and subtler states of matter and finer grades of atoms which can do the same thing? Thus a vast interlacing web would be formed in which energies or activities or substances are gradually stepped down or transmuted from the highest source of life through to the most solid and 'inert', or 'matter'.

* See *The Rosicrucian Cosmo-Conception* by Max Heindel.

The ether, in fact, would supply the explanation of those archetypal forms of which we have spoken, because one of the ethers could hold such forms in the atmosphere without interfering with all the other activities passing through it. Such mysterious possibilities indicate to us how far the human intellect will have to go before it begins really to understand the 'facts of life', and how many intricate avenues of discovery lie awaiting the scientist of tomorrow. They show us also how closely interwoven are all life's activities in that invisible world whose reality is beginning to be appreciated by us all since the advent of the radio.

Having studied the formation of the elementary hydrogen atom, the way in which radioactivity takes place, and the way in which an escaping particle can be absorbed into a finer type of atom, thus achieving transmutation, we might perhaps carry this thought a little further. Could it not be that our atoms and their particles, escaping in a long sequence of changes into ever finer and finer atoms, might eventually change into or be absorbed by an atom of the ethers, thus being transmuted into a different type of matter altogether? Could it not also be that the atoms of the ether itself are also in a state of radiation and are gradually transmuting into a still finer type of atom, forming a still more subtle substance? What could such a substance be? We are told that 'thoughts are things'. We are told that thought and emotions can often exist independent of each other, and, in fact, fight each other desperately. We know that an 'idea' can remain somewhere in the atmosphere for a long time without losing its identity, so that it can be picked up by others. Of what is it *formed?*

It is possible that even the ethers are not the last word and the ultimate fineness of the atoms of this world. Perhaps the scientist of the dim future will be studying, not radiation and transmutation in the grossest mineral forms, but the whole long ladder up which this process of evolution is mounting, through all the kingdoms of nature, until the flower of its expression unfolds in the immortal genius of man.

3

From the atom to the cell

As we know, there are certain minerals which are classed as radioactive because their activities and the changes which they undergo are spectacular and definite, and apparently self-initiated. In this connection we may ask how long, if left to itself, would a radioactive mineral atom take to reach etherealisation, to the extent of which it was capable?

In the case of uranium, which might be called the father of all the radioactive substances, it has been reckoned that a given quantity of uranium will be reduced to half its size in 4,500,000,000 years. As its radioactivity proceeds, the loss of constituents from the nucleus causes it to change from one substance to another, such as Ionium, Radon and Radium. After about fifteen of such changes it finally ends up as Radium-lead, having performed all the transmutation of which it is capable. Some of the substances have a quite different speed of radioactivity. For instance, a given quantity of Radium C will be reduced by half in fifteen millionths of a second, whereas with Radium D the time would be twenty-five years. It is good to know these facts in order to have a supple outlook on our whole question of transmutation. In any case the initial process, as it takes place naturally in the mineral world, takes untold millions of years before there is any perceptible result, even if the latter part of the radio-active process speeds itself up.

Now we can begin to question where man himself stands in relation to this vast seething world of life in which he finds himself embedded. Embedded is the right word, because the air, containing as it does about a quadrillion molecules in every cubic inch, is pressing in on him on all sides with a weight which has been reckoned to amount to about one ton! However, he has been pressed upon without being impressed! In fact he has behaved, as a general rule, like an upstart and a brigand. He has taken every liberty he chose, with the animal kingdom, with the plant kingdom, with water, with air, in fact with everything upon which he could lay his impertinent and exploiting hands.

Lastly, he has seized upon the finite bricks of the universe, the mineral atoms, in which are locked the burning, explosive and terrible forces of the Creator. With the insolence of the unaware, he is subjecting these mysterious and sacred atoms to every indignity, cruelty and outrage of which he can conceive, in order to exploit them, either in wholesale slaughter of his fellows —or the threat of it—or else in the production of false comfort and material security for a people remaining essentially underdeveloped. Man has brought upon himself untold disease, want and misery through his exploitation of soil, animal and plant. Does he expect to right it all by yet another exploitation more dangerous than all that has gone before?

By his work with nuclear energy, is he in fact helping human progress forward in ways which are in alignment with the Divine Plan, or is he getting still deeper into the Slough of Retribution? Are there other kinds of approach to the whole question of transmutation and nuclear energy, which would bring a nobler result than material benefits or material annihilation? These are the urgent and thrilling questions which demand an answer and to which we must bend all our powers of comprehension whilst there is yet time.

In nature the evolution of the mineral goes on without the production of deadly fall-out gases and other poisonous by-products; otherwise the living world had been poisoned to death long ere now. Nature's method is to arrange a symbiosis or interplay between all living things in such a way that good fertile soil, live electrified water and pure nourishing air are continually produced. The evolution of all the living forms in nature is brought about by the response of the innermost life to gentle stimuli from outside. It is the inner life which finally expands to the extent that it produces change, from the inside to the outside, due to the influence of the higher vibrations upon the lower ones. That is normal development, due to the growth of the soul in all things.

Man, however, in his haste and greed for quick results often attains his ends through producing artificial changes on the *outer* form by violent and unnatural means. He thus outrages nature, awakening a primeval resistance which expresses itself as poisonous effluvia, epidemics, blights and many other catastrophes which, ironically, he calls 'Acts of God'. By slaughtering the trees he has produced flood and soil erosion; by interfering with the rivers he has produced stagnation in the water table; by misusing the animal kingdom he has upset the economy of nature. Finally, he is attacking the very foundations of all life, the mineral atoms.

He could have expressed his genius so differently, if he had sought to understand the purpose and the design of the Creator and tried to co-operate with and help the Divine Will instead of his greedy and fearful little self.

Is it too late for him to repent and call a halt? Will the

whole world have to be devoured by fire (the flames of nuclear chain reaction) as has been prophesied? Will the end of this century see us all going blindly on our way to a spectacular nuclear annihilation?

What is going to save us—what could possibly save us from this crazy march to a futile fate? Man with his Atom Bomb is behaving like a sleeping maniac driven by a nightmare of fear. If he could wake up and discover the truth about himself and his real purpose on this planet, he might find it so enthralling that he would forget his fear and his need to stifle it with smog and sex and speed.

Let us continue, then, with our search for man's true place and task in the scheme of things.

One of the most mysterious transmutations in nature takes place when atoms have so built themselves up that out of them a living cell can come into being. We all know the details of this process from many text books. With the simple hydrogen atom as the basic brick, the sixth atom to be built up was that of carbon, containing six protons and six neutrons in the nucleus, and twelve electrons encircling it. This formation allowed of the outer electrons to link hands with those of different atoms to form a great variety of compounds of such complex character that finally that subtle substance which we know as protoplasm came into being. We can only suppose that those mysterious forces, implicit in our four ethers, arranged for this protoplasm to appear, but we do know that it was the medium which the first nuclei were able to use to build themselves the embryonic form of the first organic living creature—the animal or plant composed of one cell.

Like the atom, the cell is a tiny law unto itself, with its own polarity, its own magnetism and radiation, its own ring-pass-not. But besides its own atmosphere it possesses two things which the atom has not. These are a tiny body of protoplasm and the power to propagate itself. One-cell creatures vary enormously in complexity, character and activities. Many books have given us the long story of their evolution, and of how they help to build up all the forms of the kingdoms of nature, producing essences and juices, bone and muscle, hair and feather, the moss and the green leaf. Using the atoms and their compounds as their building material, and having access to an Intelligence which makes them past masters in architecture, engineering, chemistry, inventiveness and adaptability, the tiny cells have built up this world of living creatures without, apparently, these living creatures having a word to say in the matter. The millions of cells in the body of man are each doing highly specialised work, producing subtle organic essences, building man's body around a perfect and classic mould whose form is probably held in being by the ethers in which both man and cell are embedded, and in which, we may imagine, the frost crystal patterns are also latent awaiting a given situation.

The human being could not design or make any of the juices, bones, nerves, eyes or glands which the respective cells do so competently and inevitably. Nor, presumably, does an animal or a tree have any idea of the highly technical and scientific knowledge wielded by the cells which compose their beings.

Who, then, directs these cells? We can of course say that 'God' directs them. But then God has also given us the power to ask this question and the ingenuity to dis-cover one after another of His laws and secrets. Should we therefore be content to remain for ever more ignor-ant than the smallest cell, or can *we* also learn to tap the source of this marvellous Intelligence?

A number of scientists, such as Professor d'Arsonval,

Daniel Berthelot, Gurwitsch, Franck, Albert Noden and Georges Lakovsky, have been studying the radiations emitted by plants, insects and animals. Inasmuch as we know that a 'comparatively' inanimate thing such as a mineral atom emits radiations, we cannot be astonished to find that all more sentient creatures emit them too. It has in fact been proved that every living thing does radiate, although to a greater or lesser degree. For instance potatoes, leeks, ivy, pollen, dahlias and other familiar things were found to emit quite strong radiations. Others, as for instance the eucalyptus tree, were found to be actually radioactive. As for insects, apparently some flies, spiders and beetles 'give off an amount of radioactivity equivalent to three to fifteen times the uranium value for an equal mass'—which means that a living insect can transmute or release mineral atoms fifteen times more actively than a piece of mineral of his own size could do. In this connection we must refer to the law of nature we mentioned on page 30, by which a body of a higher vibration can attract and influence that with a lower one. Thus the plant world can influence and transmute the mineral world, the animal world can influence and transmute the plant world, whilst the 'Lord of Creation'—man—can, or could, exert the greatest transmuting influence of all.

If atoms radiate, and if an insect composed of atoms radiates, it follows that the living cell made from the atoms and composing the insect might also radiate. Georges Lakovsky has confirmed that this is the case, in his brilliant researches into the composition of the cell.

Returning for a moment to the infinitely small, we have seen that the physical atom, although composed of separate particles, each with its own oscillation and wave-length, and although containing millions of 'cosmic atoms' which each presumably vibrate also, yet emits its own *major* individual vibration and wave-length to which all its component parts are subsidiary. In the same way an insect will emit a major vibration which is its own keynote and encompasses those of all the lesser beings composing its form. The same plan holds good for a larger animal and for man himself. Composed, as he is, of millions of cells, bacteria and microbes, the human being is a symphony of vibrating notes which is orchestrated to and controlled by the one major vibratory rate which is his keynote and his signature unique unto himself.

Lakovsky has discovered that the living cell is designed in such a way that it becomes an electrical oscillating circuit. It stores electricity and emits its own specific wave-length. It is in fact a minute battery. It is tuned in to a definite vibratory rate and absorbs at its northern pole cosmic radiations of that rate. It stores them, modifies them to its own character, and re-emits them coloured by that modification. This situation is brought about because the nucleus of the cell, the chromosomes, formed of mineral conductive material, is of a shape which forms a perfect oscillating circuit. This nucleus is bathed in a liquid containing all the salts of the sea. Therefore the correct balance of positive and negative, of acid and alkali, is produced. Unconsciously man has copied this in making the ordinary electric battery. He is unaware that the same situation *must* be present in his own body for him to remain alive. His muscles provide the acid situation, his blood provides the mineral-filled alkaline situation, his whole system is that of an open electrical circuit. We have already spoken of the positive-negative pole running down his spine, through which he can absorb a variety of cosmic forces.

May we digress still further, and consider that vast

D

organism, our planet, from this same aspect? We know that it also has a living core, a north-south pole, that it has magnetic attraction, and a ring-pass-not which holds its atmosphere. It has great continents whose active living flesh of soil gives it its acid aspect, and these are bathed in the mighty oceans which provide the alkaline aspect. All those constituents which we find in the living cell, such as oil, fat, carbon, silica, are deposited in the planet. Man has dug out the coal, drained out the oil, and is, it is feared, upsetting the balance of salts in the oceans by many of his activities. What can he expect but climatic disasters when he takes such crazy liberties with the Omniscient Design?

Naturally, for a long time scientists disputed Lakovsky's discovery of the oscillation of the cell, because they said that there were no wave-lengths short or fine enough to be absorbed by such a minute circuit. But he later proved, however, that amongst the millions of cosmic rays reaching this earth there was a wave-length to fit every type of cell. He produced an instrument called the Multiple Wave Oscillator which was tuned to receive a variety of cosmic wave-lengths, and with which he could restore vitality to deficient cells. He thus performed many notable cures. This instrument was in use immediately before the 1939–45 war in hospitals in France and Italy. It was said to have produced a miraculous recovery in the Pope during his dangerous illness in 1937.

Lakovsky was also able to cure diseased plants by feeding them with cosmic rays. His researches demonstrated that the cell is a sentient entity, with its own individual life, and that this life is initiated, coloured and characterised by one of the millions of cosmic waves which is itself governed and characterised by the stellar body from which it comes. It is therefore to some great star pursuing its vast cycle of life far from our own solar system that the living cell in the body of man owes its nature. May we not conclude that it receives its intelligence and its knowledge of how to work from this source also? Or are there some smaller and nearer intelligences instructing the cell?

We have observed that the character of an atom is determined by the rate of its vibration, which is determined by the number of positive protons within its nucleus. The *rate* of vibration of a cosmic ray spells the character and quality of the orb from which it comes. We might learn something about these cosmic giants by studying the characters of the cells who receive their respective rays. It seems as if there might here be a clue to the age-old and always revered science of astrology.

After the first little living cells had appeared on this planet what did they do, in order to play their part in the plan of evolution, and help to build up a living world? The first cells were those who were to form the vegetable kingdom. One of the new capacities which they exhibited was the power to feed upon the mineral kingdom.

The mineral atom is nourished and kept alive by subtle rays and forces. In its finest and most attenuated form the mineral atom *is* the cosmic ray! But in its grosser form the mineral atom has produced crystals and then compounds, until it has become solid, 'inanimate', immovable rock, which of itself is practically unchangeable.

The living cell owes its intrinsic ethereal electrical life to the cosmic rays, but its physical body feeds upon the mineral compounds of our planetary mineral kingdom. The one-cell plant produced acids which disintegrated rock, reducing it to powder whilst releasing many elements into the air, which in time produced an atmosphere fit for the animal kingdom to breathe. The decaying bodies of the defunct plant cells mingled with the rock dust and eventually produced that magic substance, fertile soil, in which larger and larger plants were enabled to grow. Finally the lord of the plant kingdom, the tree, appeared.

The earliest plant cells banded together to form the lichens which made their first attack upon the rocks. From these small beginnings life soon flourished savagely upon the young planet, until the days of the giant ferns and vast prehistoric trees, when quantities of carbon, nitrogen, oxygen and all the other ingredients necessary for the next kingdom in nature, the animal kingdom, to come into being, were lavishly produced.

Besides manufacturing soil out of the static mineral world, the plant cell developed the power to make chlorophyl, that wonderful green substance inherent in the leaf, which is the food of millions of creatures from the tiny to the great, and which transformed the bare world into a garden of green glory.

The plant cell did not do all this work alone. At an early stage it was helped by the first little one-cell animals, who collaborated with it in a variety of ways. This partnership was faithfully upheld and developed, until at the present day the plant and the tree depend greatly upon the tiny bacteria at their roots, who begin the process of making the minerals in the soil available to the root in soluble form.

All this intricate work is helping with the transmutation of the mineral world. The grosser mineral atoms and compounds are firstly modified and refined by their passage through the bacterial digestive processes. They are still further refined by their incorporation into the sap of the plant. By this means they are lifted up out of their dark earthy prison and carried right into the rays

FROM THE ATOM TO THE CELL

of the sun. They meet with the teeming vibrational life of the atmosphere, and, blending in many happy marriages, they help to compose the miracle of the green leaf. This is not the final act, however, for their next great achievement is to help to produce the flower, the fruit and the seed. Finally, some of them spring free and issue out upon the air in their finest liberated form, as the ingredients of subtle alcohols, essences, perfumes and radiations.

The cosmic intelligence within the little cells has taught them how to differentiate themselves into bacteria cells, wood cells, leaf, flower and fruit cells, and how to work out all the various juices, structures and forms in never-ending variety and adaptability. Millions of atoms achieve their liberation from the solid physical mineral world through their service to the plant kingdom, and are set free into their parent cosmic rays once more. Millions remain with the plant world awaiting a further and a different transmutation.

This is brought about by the action of the cells which build the animal kingdom. When the animals came into being they brought to our planet two new capacities. They could move from place to place instead of being rooted in the gound as is the plant kingdom; and they were also possessed of a strong emotional feeling. We have only to watch the delight and excitement of birds when engaged in their beautiful daily tasks to be convinced of this. I remember one occasion when I threw some tempting bits of straw on to the carpet for my ring doves who had begun to build a nest in their cage. The little lady seized the straw immediately, and quivered with such excitement that for once she forgot how to find the door of the cage. After circling it in vain a few times, she landed on the top of the cage in such a state of frustrated emotion that she was violently sick! We also once possessed a tame rabbit who exhibited intense emotion and excitement, and also memory. He learnt to understand many words, and finally developed a voice!

Those who make a study of the animal world will know that the qualities of affection, devotion, fear, joy, curiosity, playfulness, humour, industry, cunning, self-sacrifice, desire and depression are all to be found in a variety of animals; and that these qualities are unevenly distributed, as in man. In fact many species of animals are liable to possess all those emotional qualities which go to make up the human character or nature. Apart from the human brain or mentality, the reactions of average people and animals are identical. The human being *is* an animal, plus something more.

Therefore, and now we come to the crux of the matter, the atoms and cells within an animal are bathed in and influenced by the effluvia or the energy of emotion. They are subjected to a new type of influence which was not present in the plant kingdom. If we consider how this influence works and what it does, we will realise that it brings about a new phase in the process of transmutation.

The ancient Wisdom explains that all the emotional life in the world functions with the help of a type of atom which is still finer than that which forms the ethers. These finest atoms form a medium or substance which has been named 'astral substance'. It is said to be so light and volatile that it is impervious to the law of gravitation. It is, however, negative and responsive to the radiations issuing from the electric personality of a living creature. It is explained that every living creature draws into its ring-pass-not sufficient etheric atoms to maintain its connection with the ethers. We are told that these atoms are built into a strong framework, permeating the body like a mesh of infinitely fine cobweb, along whose cords all the electric and radiatory forces can play. It is this living mesh, apparently, which feeds and maintains the physical atoms and cells of the body, who cling to it and are actually built upon it.

It seems marvellous that so much was postulated by the most ancient civilisations about these invisible matters, and that they expounded it so fully and explicitly. We can only accept it as hypothetical until 'proven' by modern science, but it could successfully explain many otherwise unexplainable mysteries. The Ancient Wisdom states that a living creature also draws into its ring-pass-not sufficient of the finest astral or emotional atoms to form for itself an 'astral body', or medium, or substance for the activities of the emotional nature.

The emotional world is the sphere of desire, of driving force, of the urge to do, to grow, to acquire, to experience. It is the sphere of attraction and repulsion, of love, hate, fear, excitement. The astral atoms are swept swiftly into action by the reactions of the personality to all impacts from the outer world, and by the activities of the instincts, or, in human beings, the mind. The astral atoms under such stimuli, swirl and expand until so much electric friction is produced in the aura that the individual in question can become explosive, and can be entirely 'carried away' by emotion.

So much combustion and heat can be engendered by the intensely powerful (because of a finer higher vibratory rate) astral atoms that radical changes can be brought about in the physical metabolism. The bombardment of the astral atoms can 'split' the delicate atoms of the body cells, can produce radioactivity within them, and the production of poisonous by-products, rather like scientific processes do. We know that strong emotions can set free poison in the system and can put such pressure upon the body that death sometimes takes place. It has been found that in an enraged bull, venom accumulates on his tongue which is identical with the venom of a snake. Something of the same kind takes place within the metabolism of a human being.

The astral atoms can produce and transmit heat and energy so rapidly, under stimulation, that the results seem 'miraculous'. In the heat of battle or in an emergency, people perform feats of speed or strength or endurance which would be quite impossible to them in 'cold blood'. Usually this sudden and explosive radio-activity is destructive in quality, being followed by exhaustion. However, if the emotional atoms are under the influence of beneficial radiations and stimuli they will produce a steady warmth and exhaltation which will result in a *natural* radioactivity within the cells of the body. This natural radioactivity will stream out-wards to the periphery of the body to produce what has been called the 'health aura'. These radiant particles will form in the ring-pass-not a resistance to everything inimical to the body. They will repel or neutralise unwelcome microbes, bacteria or effluvia. They play an essential part in such phenomena as fire-walking. They will thus help to render the body of animal or man impervious to disease. In a tree or plant such radiations will protect it from the attacks of pests and parasites.

This is the secret of true health. In the animal, who has no tormented and over-active mind to produce poisons within his system, the radioactivity of *radiant* health is uninhibited and plays its proper part. That is why the animal, in his natural state, enjoys almost perfect health. The emotions of the animal, except on comparatively rare occasions when he is being chased, are the normal emotions which promote growth and experience. They are not, as a rule, destructive, although of course the animal kingdom contains all sorts and conditions of character and development.

We can at once see that an atom which dwells within the body of an animal is subjected to influences which did not impinge upon it in the plant kingdom. Besides the radiations of sun and moon, heat and cold, and many of the activities of growth which were present in the plant kingdom, the atom now finds itself bathed in the emotional aura of the individual animal. The very core of its being is stimulated by the fine dancing astral atoms with their subtle penetrating powers, their quick swirling changes of action, their sudden expansions and the heat which they generate. Just as human beings today are being stimulated, refined and stretched to breaking-point by modern life with all its clamouring vibrations, so the little atom who has 'matriculated' into the animal world finds itself subjected to an intensive although beneficial education, which—and this is important—works on it gently through subtle radiations which penetrate to its *heart*. Expansion and aspiration are encouraged by this. The atom finally attains a further stage in its evolution by achieving radioactivity or an act of disintegration and reintegration into a more subtle form, producing a more subtle compound or substance within its host.

Finally, we come to the most subtly organised of all the creatures of the earth—the human being, who is, as we have remarked, an animal—plus something else. This something else is individuality, an individual mind actuated by an individual soul. All animals of one species can be guaranteed to behave, grow and react in *almost* identical ways. But man is an individual. Every person in the world is unique unto himself. He is liable to have his especial reactions to environment, to stimuli, to medicines. Children of the same parents brought up in the same conditions may be utterly different one from another. Man has a mind and brain which may either remain undeveloped or may reach unlimited powers. There is no saying under what circumstances this may take place. Man has an individual conscious soul and is able to contact something deeper still—the spiritual intelligence of the Creator.

Man has individual creative capacity. He has 'free-will', the power of choice between the mysterious duality which we call good and evil. Unlike the animals, he has the power to defy natural laws, and thus to destroy not only other beings, but himself and all he holds dear. He is thus the most complex enigma on this earth. He has spent aeons and aeons trying to read the riddle of his own existence, and of the purpose of his being. Meanwhile he has produced a medley of beauty and horror, of constructiveness and inspiration, of destruction and desecration, in which he is in danger always of losing his way entirely. He can reach heights in which he almost becomes godlike, and he can sink to grossness and brutality far below that of any animal. He knows all this, and he knows himself to be the battle-ground of forces and purposes which he is long-ing to master and to understand. Day by day his aspiration grows, and gives him no rest.

But what of the little atom which has finally matricu-lated into the body of a human being? Once again it finds itself subjected not only to all those impacts which it knew in the animal kingdom, but to a whole series of new influences as well. The astral aura of the human being is dominated by the powerful oscillation of an individual mind, which sweeps it into far greater acti-vity than it ever reached in the animal kingdom.

Violent electrical storms can be set up in the aura by human passions and fears. Terrific strains and tensions can exist within the human being, due to the 'superhuman' efforts he often makes. He can lead a life more or less in accordance with nature's plan for him, or he can do everything possible to spoil, poison and distort his own existence.

The human being is lord and master of all the atoms contained within his body and aura. They are his subjects, the prey of his tyrannies, the beneficiaries of his wisdom and good sense. According to the environment he creates for them, so will they be able to serve him. He, in his turn, is utterly dependent upon the wellbeing of his atoms. Without them the cells of his body could not be formed. The whole scheme shows a wonderful pattern of 'symbiosis', which is the name given to this interplay and interdependence.

According to the Ancient Wisdom, life is based upon a process of involution and evolution. Involution was the descent into matter, the gradual involvement of the spirit or fire of life (including atomic energy) into denser and denser forms. Evolution is the gradual conquest, by the spirit, of these dense physical forms, which are raised by the spirit through a long process of transmutation, until all will be vibrating in conscious harmony with the will of God. The purpose of all this is said to be the acquiring of the creative will—the development of a Son of God, a future ruler or guardian of some part of our universe. It has been stated that one such 'Son of God' is the great spirit which inhabits this planet, which is in fact His body. It has been suggested that every human mind constitutes a cell in *His* mind and character, so that He depends for His achievement upon the co-operation of all these units of His Being, just as on a minute scale the human being depends for his progress upon the cells of his own little mind.

Such thoughts may seem too far-fetched, even impertinent. They may appear to have little to do with our practical consideration of atomic energy. But where does science begin and where does it end? That which is 'occult magic' in one generation becomes 'scientific fact' in the next. Let us have courage to raise our eyes from the earth and consider that there *must* in any case be mighty evolutions of *some* kind proceeding in the heavens, and that it is horribly petty to conclude that only on this speck of dust called 'the earth' is anything happening! Our age-old ancestors were so much larger-minded than we are that they left us as a heritage vast archives of teaching about the cosmic spirits, their stellar bodies, and the influences both psychic and physical which they radiate everywhere and of which this earth is a recipient. Are we, sceptical and ignorant as we are today, going to turn down the findings of past geniuses, and presume to say that nothing is happening in the mighty heavens except just 'chance reactions'? Or are we going to dovetail the pattern of ancient discoveries into the pattern of modern discoveries and thus move rapidly, perhaps, towards mighty revelations?

The process of individual evolution was said to be marked by successive expansions of consciousness called Initiations. Such developments are only achieved through the fires of deep and intensive experiences, mostly self-initiated. One of these major expansions of consciousness is finally reached through the processes of pain and suffering. It is hinted that the Spirit of our planet is attaining fulfilment by this means during the long and darker ages of world history. We and the animals are said to be sharing with Him the rich experiences of pain and suffering which will lead to final liberation from the imprisonment of ignorance. From the atom upwards everything on this planet is experiencing through suffering, learning the great lesson of the oneness of all life through transgressing against it.

Therefore we have on this earth throughout all nature a situation of great complexity. On the one hand we have all the beauty, wonder, progress, love and spirituality inherent in the work of our Creator; and on the other hand we see the agony and ugliness brought about by one species preying upon another. When the lesson of creative self-reliance has been learned on this planet, the exploitation of any species by another will come to an end. 'The lion will lie down with the lamb . . . and the tiger will eat straw . . .' Would it not be sensible, until we have discovered or had proof of a better explanation of all the mysterious processes of living, at least to consider and bear in mind the postulates upon which men of genius in many of the great ancient civilisations, who have bequeathed to us much knowledge of other kinds which we fully use, based their lives?

4

What is the function of humanity?

WHEN an atom becomes part of a human being it is stimulated by that especial attribute of a human being, the thinking mind. If we have visualised the graded sequence of atoms from the dense physical atom, the etheric atoms to the astral atom, it would be logical to suppose that there is no reason that this ladder of atomic life should stop abruptly there. Would it therefore be impossible for us to concede that for the working of the mind also, atoms are needed, mental atoms of a still finer and subtler type, and with a higher, faster vibration than the emotional or astral atoms?

It is of course impossible for us to visualise or to trace atoms of such fineness, but we can for many reasons deduce that they exist. In fact, since we know that energy is convertible into atoms, that atoms are reconvertible into energy, and that most radiations are formed of atoms or atomic particles, it is impossible to deny that the radiations of the mind, which have been registered and photographed by scientists on many occasions, are composed of—or use—atoms. We are not here talking about the atoms *composing brain tissue*, but of the finer atoms which are making impressions upon that brain tissue.

As mental atoms are more potent than any atoms thus far considered, we can understand that if a man mobilised his mental forces he could control all the other grades of atoms in his body with them. This fact produced the platitude of 'mind over matter,' which acknowledges that mind can control and calm the emotions, and effect modifications in all the organs of the body and in the condition of the blood.

In fact there is no limit to what is possible when once man understands how to use his higher vibrations to control his lower ones. This is because the mind, great mystery as it is, is actually an instrument or tool organised for the use of the creative forces, the forces of will, consciousness and active intelligence. These three forces are a reflection of what we know as the Holy Trinity of God—or Will, Wisdom and Activity. Will stimulates the emotional powers and gives the irresistible urge to live and to grow. Consciousness stores memory and reflects whatever it is attuned to, passing it down to the active intelligence, which translates realisation into relevant activity. Consciousness is the soul, the mediator between spirit and person, between the invisible Cause and its embodiment.

A human being can remain completely latent and undeveloped all his life, or he can become dangerously overdeveloped. The mental atoms would be fine enough to be the nearest medium to the fire of life itself, to consciousness, to that which we call the living soul. Therefore the mind can become the medium in which the soul works, the intermediary between spirit and matter. The mind is the field of that mystery called freewill. It is the battle-ground on which is fought out the conflict between the forces of involution and evolution. It is in this fight that the embryonic human ego becomes a strong creative unit and wins freedom from imprisonment in matter. As a rule he fights blindly. But if he can achieve an enlightened outlook he will continue the struggle with joy and wonder and confidence.

The processes of involution and evolution hold the secret of 'good and evil'. They have been depicted diagrammatically as an inverted arc, a half circle whose centre dips downwards into dense physical matter. Life descends from its spiritual source until it reaches its deepest imprisonment in this earth's history at the bottom of the circle, this period covering most of what we know of human history. Having reached the bottom of the circle, involution is completed, and life then begins to mount back again to its spiritual source. This is achieved through transmutation, radioactivity in all the kingdoms of nature. Transmutation is brought about by the immense pressure of physical imprisonment, coupled with the stimulation of the core within by those radiations which can pass through the physical densities, these being, of course, the higher radiations. The higher radiations are those of the mind. It is the mind of man which is radiating all over the earth those radiations which influence all the other kingdoms of nature. The character of this influence depends on whether this instrument, the mind, is oriented to the involutionary or the evolutionary urge. Here we have the secret of good and evil—of the progressive or retrogressive.

During the descent into matter, the 'fall of man', or involution, it has been 'good' to be deeply concerned with everything physical, to develop to the full the instruments of emotion, brain and body, and the powers to influence growth and development in the mineral, plant and animal kingdoms. In order to achieve all this personal development man became very egocentric, egotistical, self-centred and shut off from the spiritual radiations. He thus created a community ruled by self-interest. Separatism, and the exploitation of everything to his own ends, was the result, producing world history as we know it.

Throughout this history, however, the future way of evolution has always been held up before mankind by the world's great spiritual teachers, so that man's inner hidden spiritual core would always be receiving that stimulation from higher vibrations which would eventually bring about transmutation.

We can understand that so long as a human being is on the involutionary downward half of the arc it is right for him to be self-absorbed and self-centred, otherwise he would never build himself into a creative individual. Nations, who also share in this process, are strongly nationalistic and patriotic during their involutionary period, and become internationally minded when they arrive at the beginning of their evolutionary stage. They are then, *as a nation*, achieving transmutation, becoming radioactive and radiating a high and progressive wavelength over the earth.

It is therefore right and good for a young embryonic nation to wish to achieve its nationhood, to go through the stages of nationalism and patriotism until it has achieved national individuality and developed that aspect of national genius peculiar to itself. If it neglected or shirked this process it would be holding back the evolution of the whole body of humanity, which needs to be perfected in its every part. Nevertheless, the influence of those older nations who have reached a higher level can help the younger nations to avoid the uglier traits of greed, exploitation and the power-lust, which accompany the earlier stages of self-development, and can infuse them with the ultimate ideal of a world brotherhood of nations. This can be done through the radioactive powers of the more evolved nations.

In considering the qualities of any being in any of the kingdoms of nature one must first try to ascertain the

E

stage at which it functions on the involutionary-evolutionary arc. That which is good and right at one stage becomes retrogressive (evil) when a more advanced stage is reached. At a certain stage in human history war is glorious, so is conquest, exploitation, and self-aggrandisement. At one stage and place polygamy is 'right'. At one stage slavery was considered 'right'. The common usage of one period becomes during evolution the crime of a later period. Mankind, through realisation, is moving ever nearer to a concept of the oneness of all life, of its interdependence, of the fact that the welfare of all depends upon the welfare of each one. Such movements as the League of Nations, the United Nations, the Atlantic Charter, and all the other 'world' movements, are actuated by the radioactive rather than the conservative qualities. The growing awareness of man's exploitation of the animal and the plant kingdoms is also due to his increasing radioactivity, and his gradual release from the prison of self-centredness.

This brings us to the consideration of the actual place and function of mankind in the picture of world evolution.

The human being possesses the power deeply to affect every type of life upon this planet. His inventive mind has enabled him to experiment and to perform actions which can defeat to a certain extent the plans and designs of nature. Certain natural laws, which are irrevocable and inevitable in their outworking, will defeat him in the end. He cannot upset nature's arrangements and permanently get away with it. But he can do a dangerous amount of mischief and work a great toll of destruction, even if he himself is included in the destroyed. Climatic disasters such as floods, fires, earthquakes, would appear to be catastrophic in their effects. But the earth does recover from them. Greenery comes again and it is merely a question of time before nature smiles beneficently once more.

But the destructive works of man have permanent results. He has extinguished many species of animals. He has created, since earliest times, deserts and soil erosion to such an unnatural extent that nature has been defeated by him, and has been unable to heal the scars thus perpetrated. The deserts and dust-bowls are examples of this. When once such a 'loss of skin' has taken hold, it spreads like a cancer. The desert of Sahara is encroaching by thirty miles every year. The dust-bowls of America, created before men's eyes in the generations of this century, have frightened them at last into taking drastic action to repair the damage.

Mankind has shown that he has the power to destroy this planet through soil erosion (flaying alive), by polluting the air, water and soil with noxious, unnatural chemical compounds, upsetting the animal economy by killing off some and overbreeding other species, and in a hundred ways bringing discomfort and defeat to the beneficient spirit who informs this great atom, our earth. Man has suffered and is suffering horribly as a result of all this. He is riddled with disease, physical and mental, and his life span is sadly reduced. It is impossible to guess to what extent his actions have affected the climate and all other conditions on this planet. He is at present playing with fire (atomic fire) to an extent which could and may change the atmosphere of this earth and disrupt all the fundamental arrangements which make normal life possible.

So far in his history man has acted, in general, more destructively than otherwise on the physical plane, whereas he could have acted entirely constructively and in harmony with the plan for evolution. For, inasmuch as he possesses, as we have seen, powers of destruction far greater than any other creature on earth, he can, by the same token, wield the blessed powers of healing, construction and enlightenment to at least the same extent. No one can tell what a fairyland he could have made of this planet if he had worked hand in hand with the Divine Designer.

As things are, it would take man a thousand years to repair the damage he has caused, so that the bounty of nature could have full play and all her children be well provided for. Therefore the sooner humanity awakens to the situation and begins the work of restitution, the less lengthy and impossible will be the task. The joyful fact is, indeed, that countless people all over the world are becoming aware of this situation, and have actually begun on various aspects of reparation. Not only that, but they are linking up with each other across the earth in the warm brotherhood which such work brings and which cuts clear through all barriers of class, culture, creed, race and politics.

It is plain, therefore, that from the objective point of view mankind holds a potent and unique place in the world scheme. By using his brain and his hands he can aid and encourage right growth and development in all the kingdoms of nature, including his own. He can adapt his genius and all his discoveries in ways that will *not* go against natural laws and which will not take liberties with the economy of the planet. Such work would be absorbing and fascinating in the extreme, far more so than much of the guesswork and error with which he is involved whilst under a different and more egotistical orientation.

For instance, he has not found out how to obtain atomic energy except at vast expense, vast effort, great uncertainty and danger, and entailing the production of horribly poisonous by-products. Yet the more ancient civilisations and the Alchemists of the Middle Ages possessed many profound postulates in regard to the production of elixirs and energies and the achievement of transmutations, without either great expense, vast paraphernalia or the production of dangerous by-products. It is suspected that such races as the early Egyptians used radioactive substances in the sealed-up tombs of their Pharaohs, which were calculated to deal destruction to future desecrators. Apparently also such ancient races were able to light subterranean tombs and passages by the use of some mysterious radiation for which archaeologists cannot account. There are paintings on the ceilings in which colours have been graded so delicately that a strong light must have been used, yet any naked flame would have blackened the work. In such enterprises as the building of the Pyramids and other ancient monuments the builders were able to wield an amount of power which is still quite a mystery to modern engineers.

As for the mediaeval Alchemists, there is a great deal of circumstantial evidence from which we can deduce that some of them did perhaps achieve phenomenal results in the sphere of transmutation and radioactivity, results which would have been of profound interest to modern scientists.

Throughout history, therefore, there have been periods when the knowledge of the existence and potency of the atoms engaged the geniuses of the time, and was productive of many experiments and much literature.

However, there is one great difference between the approach of the modern scientist to atomic energy and that of the ancient savant. The modern scientist is entirely materialistic, physically based and objective both in his outlook and in his experiments. By this I mean that he leaves out the possibility of any actual relationship between his mind and its atomic energy with the mineral atomic energy which he wishes to manipulate. Although in dealing with mineral atomic energy he is dealing with radiation, electricity, combustion, stimulation, heat and energy, and although he knows by now that his mind works by reason of and is composed of these same ingredients graded in a higher scale of wave-lengths, he has not yet seen the possibility of using the higher to control its lower counterpart. In other words, he has left out of his laboratory the most subtle and powerful of all his available instruments— his own mind, considered not as a thinking medium but as an active electrical instrument.

The ancient savants, on the contrary, not having developed our objective 'scientific' approach, were far more conscious of the one electrical instrument they possessed—the mind. They knew how to produce a dynamic situation by blending the electrical rays of the mind with the storage powers of the breath, and with the radioactive vibrations of the voice, and even with the catalystic radiations of colour. By these means they achieved many results which are puzzling and inexplicable to the 'hard-headed' scientist of today, who apparently prefers to risk blowing up the planet by less subtle methods.

It is quite probable that in time he will come upon some of the fundamental laws, and will produce the *Second* Atomic Age, when energy, power and transmutation will be produced harmlessly, by the use of colour, sound and the most potent instrument of all— the trained human dynamo. By such gently powerful means he will be able to obtain his results, if he so wishes, without using violence on any kingdom in nature, and therefore without arousing resentment expressed as poisonous by-products. It was this possibility which was realised by the thinkers of many old civilisations. But as such knowledge would be dangerous if used with the wrong motives, a veil of secrecy was always kept closely around every approach to it.

Just as there are many ways of wielding power by purely physical means, so are there also many ways of wielding it with the mind. We are now working our way towards the very core of our subject, the sphere of cause and effect. The mind is, after all, only an instrument, although an invisible one. It is not the *cause* of activity, it is the expression of that cause. The cause lies back and beyond it. It is the will or orientation of the essential life spark, the spiritual essence of the living creature. In man the spiritual motive power has to control a complex situation which we call consciousness and which is built upon and out of memory. Without memory consciousness and mental activity of the human type could not exist. But memory is far more comprehensive and complex than would at first appear. Much that is atavistic develops in the growing mind, so that it seems to be formed in layers, of fully conscious, partly conscious, subconscious and superconscious. Memory makes the mind, and produces reactions good and bad. The human being can, if he wishes, rely entirely on drawing conclusions from and basing his actions upon his personal memory. This obviously limits him to the potentialities of only one individual. But actually this is only a fraction of the possibilities within his grasp.

The human mind is, in its invisible formation, a wireless instrument; that is to say it is capable of tuning in to an unlimited range of vibrations or to be plugged in, as it were, to act as a receiving channel or a link with other mental radiations outside of itself. Not only that, but the mind *through its own radioactivity* can achieve transmutation by means of which it can channel itself to vibrations of a higher potency than the mental, a potency to which we have given the name of 'spiritual'. By this we mean that which is nearest to and most identical with the Divine Intelligence and Will of the Creator Himself.

At his highest state of awareness the human being is capable of receiving and interpreting instructions, information and illumination of a higher grade than that obtainable from any of his fellow-men, however superior. Much of such wisdom and information, handed down through the generations of ancient primitive tribes, is of a character not only far beyond the mental capacities of the receivers, but even too profound and far-reaching for most of the advanced thinkers of today. Therefore this channel of communication with what we may call the Universal Mind has always been open to mankind. Not only that, but, just as the animal-human capacity for sensitivity to radiations—radar—has been blunted by 'civilisation', so also is his receiving instrument to the all-permeating Intelligence blunted if compared, in certain ways, with many of his savage ancestors.

In general, man appears to have developed his external and objective capacities, his 'civilised' and commercialised existence, at the expense of his real individual and potential self. He has allowed his creations to go far ahead of their creator. This has produced an unbalanced state of affairs because now he is governed by them. He and his fellows are committed to an atomic armament race because they rely on atomic arms, instead of on their own intelligence and goodwill, to develop better conditions and relationships.

When a majority of egocentric individuals produce in their totality a set of egocentric nations, the policies and practices of those nations are bound to be involutionary, i.e. self-protective, self-insulating, acquisitive, exploitive. We have seen this picture throughout history. When a given percentage of individuals in a nation have broken out of the cage of self-centredness, and become world-centred and uninsulated, they produce in their nation the beginnings of internationalism, humanitarianism and spiritual statesmanship. Recently we have seen these things happening. The League of Nations and the Atlantic Charter heralded the beginnings of the change.

When a majority of selfless and progressive individuals have emerged in any nation, that nation will lead the way towards a new Golden Age. We may look around with interest, and wonder which will be the first nation to achieve such fulfilment and adulthood. Such a pioneer nation will be ready to suffer loss, and to relinquish cherished objectives. She may have to face humiliation, scorn, misunderstanding even, at the hands of those who have not yet sensed the new inevitable orientation. Something of such a situation has perhaps been observed by us during recent years.

In the light of our present studies we must accept as right and inevitable both those younger, or regenerating, nations who are anxious to develop nationally and independently, and those older ones who begin to show a mysterious willingness to 'fail' as empire builders and to forget the words 'in the national interest'.

If the barriers of self-interest between nations were finally to go down, possibly a great relief would be felt by the entity who informs this planet. It must surely give discomfort to such an entity if the members of his body war against each other or are trying to exploit each other. How shall it benefit him that one of his arms (speaking figuratively) seeks development at the expense of the other, or that one limb should be overfed whilst another starves? Surely the whole electrical 'blood circulation' of the planet is restricted and upset by such situations, and also therefore all his emanations, which we know as 'climate'?

In the early days of man's history, we are told that the planetary Deity, utterly distressed by humanity's behaviour, decided to cleanse the planet by Flood. Having thus washed from his skin those human creatures who should have been earth's greatest helpers but had become instead destructive parasites, those few were spared who were most worthy to make a fresh start. What happened? No sooner were they on dry land again than they offered up a burnt sacrifice—they began to slay once more. And the Deity said (Genesis viii, 21), 'I will not again curse the ground any more for man's sake; for the imagination of man's heart is evil from his youth. . . .' In the next chapter, whilst giving His instructions, the Deity says: 'But the flesh with the life thereof, which is the blood thereof, shall ye not eat. And surely your blood of your lives will I require . . .; at the hand of every beast will I require it, and at the hand of every man's brother will I require the life of man.'

From the beginnings of its history the Christian religion, as well as the Jewish, had forbidden the killing of both man and beast. The first chapter of Genesis makes it quite clear that the trees were to provide the food of man, and his work was to tend them; and that the green herbs were the food for animals. But after the slaying of Abel, mankind went from bad to worse, and the animals shared in this corruption and many took to violence also. 'And God looked upon the earth, and behold, it was corrupt; for all flesh had corrupted his way upon the earth. And God said unto Noah, "The end of all flesh is come before me; for the earth is filled with violence through them; and behold, I will destroy them with the earth".'

The mysteries of the scriptures are open to much argument and misinterpretation. We can turn really more safely to science to get at the truth. Not until the king of the plant world, the tree, had come into growth was man able to appear on this planet. Before this, the animal kingdom, whose food was the green herb, had flourished plentifully. When, later, the thoughts of early mankind turned evil, greedy and violent, we now realise that the earth's atmosphere must have been quickly permeated by them, and that their 'wireless' radiations coursed around the globe and were picked up by all those types of creatures who shared with a man a certain tendency to *activity* which is always associated with the acid or positive aspect. It may be that this influence caused them to become carnivorous and to begin to prey upon the more alkaline and peaceful type of creatures.

It is interesting to note in this respect that one of the first reactions of progressive people of this epoch is to feel a strong responsibility towards remedying the persecution by man of the animals, and also to abhor the slaughtering of one species by another. So much so, that animal-lovers are succeeding in demonstrating the possibility of rearing carnivorous animals such as cats, and omnivorous animals such as dogs, in perfect health and spirits upon a vegetarian diet. There has even been a much publicised case recently of a lioness who had brought herself up as a vegetarian while living as a member of a human household. Many people have also acknowledged the biological fact that the human being is a frugivorous species. All such viewpoints, when held in increasing numbers, constitute a new and different radiation in the earth's atmosphere, and one which impinges upon the consciousness of all living creatures and which must finally colour the consciousness of the planet as a whole.

At first the idea of a thinking, feeling planetary Entity may seem far-fetched. However, scientists are now getting to the point of admitting the existence of a tremendous vitality, an evolutionary cycle, and a type of consciousness within the atom, and a still more individual character and consciousness within the organic cell. If they can go thus far in the case of such minute bodies, why should they not concede a conscious sentiency to the larger atom, our planet, built as it is upon the same scheme of electrical polarity as is the atom, the cell and man, and having regard also to the fact that the mind and feelings exist and function through electrical media?

Indeed, as we mentioned, the Ageless Wisdom teaches that the human being plays the part of a mind-cell and brain-cell to the planetary Entity. Just as the tree cannot obtain its nourishment without the intervention of the bacteria at its roots, so, possibly, the mental activity of the planet cannot affect the kingdoms of nature without using man as its intermediary or thinking instrument.

Thus the spirit of the planet, which to us is as a Deity, may depend completely, in a certain respect, on the human being for the achieving of development, progress and transmutation for the planet as a whole.

This is an awe-inspiring thought. It is not one which we can possibly dismiss out of hand. We know that all life is wonderfully interdependent, and based on the principle of symbiosis or 'give and take'. It is illogical to claim that this all-permeating principle is cut off sharply when one comes to mankind, and that he has no relationship whatever with the planet whose activities are so beautifully adapted to make life possible for him. It is surely also foolish to claim that there can be no purpose behind the fact that man possesses an intellect with apparently unlimited powers of various kinds, and that he is able to 'plug in', if he so trains himself, to a Universal Intelligence which can confer on him a superhuman power and awareness.

5

The cell-genius at work

THE cells are the little bricks which make up the edifice of a plant, an animal or a man. They build themselves up with the help of the fine outer cosmic radiations; the radiations of our sun and solar system which are of a grade different to the cosmic rays; the radiations of our own planet and its satellite the moon, which are of yet other grades; and the grosser mineral atoms which inhabit the earth. All this range is composed of atoms of the same series of elements and their energy radiations. The only difference is of fineness, quality or degree.

The pattern of the whole shows a ladder of infinite gradations, the stepping down from the subtlest and most high-powered atomic vibrations, which are the nearest to the original spiritual or causative influence, right down to the grosser atom of this planet. The latter is in reality a molecule of cosmic atoms, but is considered at present by scientists to be the ultimate atom from which molecules of solid matter are formed.

We cannot yet understand the inscrutable Purpose which caused mineralised spirit and energy to become congealed, imprisoned and hardened into heavy mineral rock, as well as the lesser degrees of solidity which hold the spirit of plant, animal and man; nor yet the spiritual and cosmic impulses which play upon earthly imprisonment until the spirit within is sufficiently stimulated to break through into radioactivity and transmutation. We cannot see the reason for it all. But we can watch and detect this whole procedure in action. We can perceive that it is indeed a way of liberation into future freedom and potency; the way, perhaps, towards unimaginable experience and fulfilment and revelation.

The little genius who makes it all possible is the living organic cell. There came a moment in history when the cell first produced itself as a single complete entity, a one-cell animal or a one-cell plant. This was the miracle of the first act of creation in nature. In order to prepare the ground for this, however, the world of mineral atoms had been very busy, dancing into partnerships and marriages which produced ever more subtle compounds and more response to and reaction with the cosmic and systemic (solar-system) radiations.

Finally, the point was reached when the waiting life impulse was able to gather to itself these subtilising minerals, fix them electrically to the waiting archetypal cell patterns in the ether and crystallise them into the first living sentient cell bodies. The fascinating mystery of how and why this first happened is one of the riches in store for questing mankind. At present we can but piece together the information so far available, and deduce from it what we may.

Physical life has been built up through a process of differentiation or division into a long series of units, of which each species has different qualities, attributes and effects. The first of these differentiations resulted in the creation of the positive and negative, the male and female principles. The second differentiation, as we have seen, gave us the neutron, the clamping together of male and female into a state of crystallisation and of weightiness. From these basic bricks a vast series of combinations was built up, just as the whole of music is built up from the seven basic notes.

Each element thus produced, such as iron, or gold, has its individual vibratory number, its spectroscopic colour, its chemical quality and its effect on or relationship with all other substances. The series of elements can be likened to musical scales. Further differentiations are achieved through the marriages of the elements to make compounds. These can be likened to the musical chords. From the basic component parts whole symphonies of music and of life can be built up.

Every plant and every animal on the earth belongs to its one special classification or species. This we know from its outward form, but from our present studies we can realise that there must be an inner classification of vibration and therefore of character and quality which would give us much more profound insight and meaning in our work of classifying. Let us consider how what it is that originates the differing qualities of living creatures. We must begin, of course, with our solar system, looking upon it as it really is—a large atom! Scientists may soon begin to suspect that the solar system itself is spinning *as a whole globe* round its own axis; and is revolving in an orbit around an infinitely greater solar system.

The radiations and mineral particles of the whole cosmic universe are impinging upon our solar system and building it up into a solar atom. It has its proton or central positive core, the sun, and its electrons or planets, each revolving in its respective stratum of the sun's atmosphere or ring-pass-not. Each planet revolves at a different distance from the sun, therefore experiencing a different state of heat, atmospheric pressure, magnetism and radiation. This produces in each of the planets their variations in size, weight, speed and composition. But there is a further factor of the utmost importance which comes into the composition of the planets. All the cosmic mineral radiations pour into the receiving end of that great electrical battery, the solar atom. They are radiated and distributed by the positive sun and gathered and stored by the negative electrons, the planets. But the aforementioned different situation of each planet causes it to attract and absorb one mineral radiation more than all the others. Although it may absorb the whole cosmic gamut, nevertheless each planet is differently attuned by reason of its position, and therefore it receives the particles and vibrations of one particular mineral in greater quantity than all others, becoming in its *totality* an expression of that mineral.

Thus the planet Mars is so attuned, by reason of its heat, speed, size and vibratory rate, that it absorbs more of the iron radiations than do any of the other planets. Although of course many other activities and combinations of minerals take place within its sphere, it becomes an expression of the qualities and reactions of the element iron above all else. Its radiations as they impinge on all the other planets in our solar system, including our earth, give out the iron which it has been busily storing, and give it out in the form of slightly larger and more compound atoms, built from the finer cosmic atoms which it received. This is part of the work of crystallisation or materialisation. The radiations from the planet Mars, therefore, bring us iron in a free and highly potentised form which acts as a catalyst and stimulant to all the more solid or crystallised iron already in existence on this planet.

By the same token the planet Venus, by reason of its conditioning, absorbs more cosmic copper than anything else, and so becomes the negative electron absorber of copper, and reradiates that copper to the earth.

F

As for the sun, lord of its system, it claims the lord of all minerals for its own expression, and this of course is gold.

The study of the mineral composition of the planets and of their vibratory influence upon each other is naturally a deep and extensive one. It must also include the understanding of the reactions set up in the ethers where such radiations intersect at different angles and in the different strata of the atmosphere. Each of these occurrences provides a different situation for the formation of various marriages into chemical ccmpounds, which in their turn continue the building up of an infinite variety of living substances.

The knowledge of these varying atmospheric conditions was available to savants of ancient civilisations and upon it they built up the world-wide and age-old science of astrology. In early history this science was the father of both astronomy and medicine. It was thus applied by all the ancient peoples according to their aptitude. It was an intrinsic part of both government craft and priest-craft. It was usually represented in mythical language and symbol which served to veil and protect it from mob familiarity, much as medical and legal language does today.

The ancient teachings claimed that man himself is built in certain ways on much the same pattern as the solar system or atom; that he has a central proton or sun, the heart; that he has seven major planets or electrons, the seven major glands; and that the mineral electrical radiations between all of them, working, as we have said, along the channels provided by the ether, build up the subtle chemical compounds from which his tissues are formed.

Furthermore, they claimed that each man's principal 'planets' or glands was governed or fed by its respective counterpart in the solar system, because each gland owed its character to a certain mineral and its compounds. We know that there is definitely some truth in this, as copper, iron, silica and other minerals are each allocated to work in their respective organs within the body. As we have said, these minerals can be relayed to them from the atmosphere by the use of coloured glass, by the use of coloured lights, or by the use of metal instruments so built that they absorb the cosmic radiations.

It has been possible for us to piece together a number of the ingredients which produce a situation in which the creation of living creatures can take place. Into this complex picture finally appears the little living organic cell. It is upon this minute, tender and defenceless little creature that the whole panorama of life is going to depend. The vast kingdom of the plants, the array of insect and animal species, the mysterious triumph of the human race—all these have been built and developed, modified and designed and adapted by the genius of the tiny cell. Having achieved the miracle of bringing himself into existence, the little cell took up the task of building with consummate skill the whole teeming world of life upon this planet. Informed by an Intelligence which was supreme before ever the first wondering human being began to use his brain, the humble, patient and terrifyingly clever cell surely contains in its small sphere a link with and a channel to the Creator and His Plan for this complex universe.

6

How the mind works

ONE of the age-old principles which were used as a basis for the study of life was that of the 'macrocosm and the microcosm'='As above, so below!' This held that in nature the archetypal designs and patterns repeated themselves from the infinitely great to the infinitely small. When therefore one knows the basic designs and forms, one can find one's way through all the intricacies of life both visible and material, and invisible and causative.

One of these main basic patterns is that of a solar system. We see it exemplified in our own system and in the atoms of all the elements. When we come to the living cell this pattern is not quite so easy to perceive but it can be found. The chromosomes of the cell form the proton or central sun and also produce the situation of an oscillating electric circuit for the reception of radiations of a given wave-length. The substances in the body of the cell play the part both of the negative electrons and of the mineral-filled atmosphere, which in the cell's case is composed of a liquid containing all the salts of the sea. The conditions thus set up in the cell makes its proton a positive ruler of its own little planetary system.

As a planetary system, it becomes, according to rule, negative to the greater bodies to which it gives allegiance, which are, firstly, the cosmic ray from the stellar body to which it is attuned, and secondly, the living creature in whose body it has its place.

When we come to consider the human being we find the ancient statement that man is the epitome of the whole of the universe, that he is the microcosm which repeats and reflects not only the whole of the solar system, but the history of all creation as well. From the one-cell animal and plant, the story of the creation of the plant and animal kingdoms is recapitulated within the body of man in the most extraordinary way, not only in the developing embryo but in many other respects.

The subtleties, complexities and designs within the human body are remarkable enough when considered on their own by the materialistic scientist. But when understood as an interacting repetition of all that takes place in nature both physically and subjectively or 'spiritually' the human being is seen as in fact the greatest living mystery and wonder. He contains a replica of the whole universe within himself and therefore is intimately a part of it all. By the same token he *could* have the power to influence it all, should he sufficiently develop himself as a broadcasting instrument. We can therefore begin to realise what was meant by calling man the 'son of God', a God in the making. Although still in his infancy, or only partially developed, his potentialities are illimitable.

There is yet another wonderful phenomenon which must be mentioned. Man contains in his own form a parent 'solar system' which is found within the head, and its offspring 'solar system' which is found within the body. Whilst the human embryo is forming, the head is the first thing to take shape. Within the head the pattern of the human body is formed before it is projected outwards in embryonic growth. There is the tree of life formed by the roots, trunk and branches of the arterial and nervous system. This represents man's affinity with the plant kingdom. There are the seven satellite glands around their ruling gland or proton, which gives man's affinity with the atom and the solar system. The proto-type of man, which exists first within his skull, builds his body into a larger repetition, each brain-gland control-ling and ruling its replica in the body as adequately as the individual's characteristics will permit.

Man's royal prerogative, the human mind and brain, is or should be governed by the king-gland or sun-gland, the pineal, which is the organ of his godship, and provides his channel not only to the almighty Intelli-gence, but to the spiritual-chemical rays of the sun. These rays pour into their receiving station, the pineal gland, in which and by which they are distilled into a glandular elixir, a most magical juice. This secretion passes downwards through all the other glands of the body, where it is used in the process of compounding the secondary glandular secretions. It stimulates and inspires the glands of the body to build up the human form according to the blue-print made ready by the prototype glandular system in the head.

The workers who actually accomplish this task are the living organic cells of the body. Without them nothing could be done. First of all they have to build their own bodies. This they achieve and produce themselves to form a long series of different cell species, each one adapted to do a different task. These tasks are, firstly, to build up a gland and the organ which it controls and secondly, to build all the subsidiary parts, of bone, flesh, blood, hair, and brain tissue.

The glandular system in the head controls and builds its replica in the body. The pineal sun or proton gland builds up the sun gland in the body. This is the spleen, the receiver of sunshine. The organ with which it is associated is the heart. The rest of the seven major glands form the human solar system. Each one is the vassal or subject of one of the seven planets; that is to say that a gland contains and uses more of the mineral of its ruling planet than any other.

However, it is even more complex than that. We have to take into account that the rays from the planets marry with each other and produce subtle compounds which are used by the cells who are stimulated by these fine rays which act as catalysts, causing the cells to attract and precipitate the respective minerals from the blood-stream, forming them into cell-salts for their especial use. This subject, of course, would require a book in itself, so we can only give one or two indications in regard to our subject today. For instance, the marriage of sulphur and potassium, as it takes place during the radiatory reactions coming from the planet Mercury, forms a compound from which oil originates. The gland which we know as the pancreas is 'governed' by Mercury, and therefore to the cells which compose it is allocated the fabrication of that most precious and vital of all substances, oil. The pancreas, together with its organ, the solar plexus, works with the cell-salt sulphate of potassium to ensure the proper lubrication of the whole body. The appendix is really a little reservoir for oil for the bowels. Another example is that of iron, which is precipitated into a salt by marriage with phosphorus. Thus it can be utilised by the cell for a further association with oxygen. This produces, as we know, that living red 'rust' which gives us the red corpuscles of the blood. Then again we have the important element of lime, one of the substances especially distributed through the planet Saturn. Lime forms three different marriages, one with phosphorus, one with fluorine and one with sulphur, each of which is used by appropriate cells for the making of either bone, elastic tissue or the very skins of the cells themselves. From a knowledge of the laboratory work enacted by the various cells of the body, the science of Biochemistry has been built up. This entails the preparation of replicas of the cell-salts used by the body, in a form sufficiently fine (highly triturated) to be capable of immediate absorption. Thus, since most illnesses are due to deficiencies or unbalance of the cell-salts, it is possible to aid the re-establishment of correct metabolism by a supply of the missing cell-salts. In nature these cell-salts are made available to the animal kingdom by the plant kingdom. The animal (including man) is not capable of assimilating minerals in their 'raw' state. Nor, for that matter, is the plant. The mineral molecules in the soil are split up by the bacteria at the roots of plants, sufficiently finely for them to become soluble in water, in which state they can be absorbed by the plant roots. Within the plant, the minerals undergo a further refining influence, until the cells of the plant, actuated by their respective cosmic rays, can compound them into the cell-salts from which all the various juices, oils, fibres and other substances of the plant are made.

When the human being feeds upon the plants, fruits and seeds, he obtains all the cell-salts which he requires. But what is it that enables him to utilise them? It is the cells of his body, who, actuated by their respective cosmic rays and their subtle mineral combinations, draw into themselves the particular minerals to which they are attuned, and with which they are to produce the most complicated and amazing glandular essences of so many kinds. However, the cells in the human body are not able to utilise the mineral salt-compounds as they come to them straight from the plant. Like the plant, they need intermediaries. They depend, there-fore, upon a mixed host of bacteria and virus who dwell in the blood stream, and who feed first upon the mineral-compounds until they have refined them still further so that they can be absorbed by the cell. When mineral deficiencies occur, these bacteria get out of hand through malnutrition, and draw their needs from the cells themselves, thus causing so-called disease.

Deficiencies will occur when the human being in question uses up too much of one or more minerals through over-activity of the mental or emotional impulses. These impulses, being electrical, can literally burn up the delicate chemical juices, or, through com-bustion, change their character altogether, so that poisonous substances come into being. We can see here what is meant by 'mind over matter'. The changing of the chemistry of the body by the impulses of the mind is a scientific fact. It can be performed either uncon-sciously or deliberately.

It should now be clear to us by what stages the 'solid' mineral molecules are gradually transmuted in nature. Iron by itself, or calcium or phosphorus, have no like-ness or relationship at all with the living organic sub-stances which they take part in producing. Where is the link between their whirling mineral atoms and living, breathing flesh? This link is produced by a combina-tion of circumstances designed most wonderfully by the Creator. We have shown how the atmosphere is criss-crossed by rays from the different planets, which, by reason of the constant movements in the solar system, are in process of intersecting each other at various angles and under various atmospheric pressures and tempera-tures. Such intersections form a kind of stress, strain or stimulation, something like an electric shock, which in fact shocks the atoms in the vicinity into activity. They form marriages with each other and thus a compound of one or more elements comes into being.

As these finer atoms and their compounds are drawn nearer to the earth they crystallise or harden until at last they can be considered as solid matter, however tenuous. It is these subtle compounds which can be utilised by the plant cell to act as catalysts upon the cruder minerals rising up in the sap. Let us not forget that the former are the beginnings of crystallisation of the actual cosmic rays, and that we have here an example of what we have said about the higher vibrations affecting the lower ones and being able to manipulate them.

The ancient savants would appear to have possessed a profound knowledge of all the angles and intersections produced by the cosmic rays and the types of influences thus initiated. They mapped them all out most thoroughly, producing therefrom a science which we know as astrology. As the basis of their circular map they divided the heavens up into twelve portions somewhat like the divisions of an orange. These twelve divisions were called the Signs of the Zodiac. The qualities and influences of each Sign or division were intensively studied. The effect which the different planets of our solar system exerted as they passed through these Signs and stimulated them was closely watched. The angles at which their radiations struck each other at any given moment was mapped, and the complex influences which were thereby radiated on to the earth were described with much authority.

The conviction was held that any given mineral substance or ray can express itself as a colour-quantity, sound, form and psychological influence, depending on the degree to which its atoms are transmuted, and of course, the organ of perception brought to bear upon it.

As these scholars of old were primarily interested in the *psychological* influences of the planetary radiations, they gave to them the names of deities both animal and human. They considered, in fact, that a deity was the embodiment of a psychological influence, the entity that inhabited a planet, and the pulsating life essence at the core of a major radiation.

We do not know if modern science considers itself in a position definitely to deny the possible validity of such assertions; or if it is rapidly nearing something of the same conclusions under a different guise. The wonder of it all is—where did those ancient savants of ten thousand or more years ago obtain their knowledge, and their profound postulates, right or wrong? What instruments or methods of calculation did they have which enabled them to map out the complete cycles of zodiacal changes over periods embracing hundreds of thousands of years? How could they assess the minute radiatory intersections in the atmosphere produced from moment to moment? Such work was very different from the sometimes amateurish and somewhat cheap methods of the 'astrologer' of today, and should not be confused with it.

Realising, as we now do, that the mind is an electrical instrument with attributes which resemble both the radio and radar, we can understand more readily, not only the effects which cosmic rays might have upon the mind, but the way in which the mind itself might act as a miniature cosmic ray of unpredictable influence. The fact is that the human mind is an instrument of great potency if it is one-pointed or 'whole'. Its power can be like that of a burning-glass, boring its way through to its objective.

But the average mind is not whole. It is divided against itself in a variety of ways. That part of the mind of which we are most conscious we call the concrete mind; that which deals with our daily life. It is, in fact, a concretion, a crystallisation of many memories. These memories are the records of all the instructions we have received since babyhood and all other influences which have impinged upon us. They are etched upon our mental apparatus just like a set of gramophone records. Each record will play itself, when stimulated by a mental electric shock or 'button-pressing'. Continual reaction to a memory sets up a series of reflexes to which we react almost unconsciously.

For instance, we see a man selling newspapers. A series of reflexes causes us to take out our money and buy one, almost automatically. Furthermore, if our politics are to the Right, we will react to the news conditioned by our right-thinking records within our mental apparatus, which play over certain sentences or attitudes or platitudes as soon as the political bell-push is pressed. We imagine that we are 'thinking' when we play them over. We are not performing the creative act of real thinking at all. In fact some people never do. We are simply living as automatons if we rely entirely on the playing of mental records. It is disconcerting to realise that most of us can live for days on end, perhaps talking incessantly, without thinking one thought that is original to ourselves, but merely repeating parrot-like from our store of records.

That, then, is our concrete mind. It is also concrete in that we use it to form a hard shell around our consciousness, a sort of chrysalis within which we feel safe and which is our possession and our tool for living. This chrysalis of ready-made 'thought' saves us from thinking afresh. It is our bank-balance of mental possessions. Like the snail within his shell, we use it to protect our nakedness or ignorance, to shield us against any new ideas or attitudes which might force us to make any changes. If we are lazy we will settle into a mental rut, and rely permanently upon the first concretion of ideas we built up. If we have an 'enquiring mind' or are perhaps greedy, we will continue to accumulate facts about many things as hard as we can, so that our mental possessions eventually clutter up our thinking apparatus completely.

The region of the concrete mind is that stratum of our consciousness which functions in the lowest or coarsest of mental vibrations. It is controlled by the posterior lobe of the pituitary body, which lies back of the root of the nose. In a great many people this is the only part of the mind which ever functions—the mind of 'memory', living on so-called 'facts'.

There is another region, however, which we call the abstract mind. This functions in a higher and more subtle vibration altogether. It is the medium wherein ideas take shape as opposed to facts, where an appreciation of beauty and of quality, of the arts and sciences, and of abstract conceptions can function. The gland in control of this part of the mind is known as the frontal lobe of the pituitary body.

This important organ is the receiver of impressions of many kinds. If it is underdeveloped it will receive only crude and simple impressions. But there is no limit to its powers of development. It can grow more and more sensitive and subtilised, and become the receiving station for ever higher and finer vibrations. It is the seat wherein clairvoyance and clairaudience can function. That is to say that if the five senses themselves develop so that we acquire extra-sight (somewhat like X-ray) and extra-hearing, the results can be received and registered by means of the pituitary body. It is therefore connected with what we know as psychic phenomena. When a horse or a cat 'sees' ghosts or phenomena invisible to man, or reacts to radar influences, it is using the pituitary body, which is highly developed in some animals.

We possess, therefore, a divided mind, the concrete and the abstract. But a man can possess both of these fully functioning, without being creative or original. There is some further part of the mind, back of all this, which can do the 'real thinking'. In creative thought, two or three facts or memories are contemplated. These are the elements or simple constituents of the mental laboratory. The creative mind turns its fire upon them, and fuses them into a new compound—an idea or an inspiration—so that something comes into being which did not exist before. This idea or compound may have been formed by other minds before, but when an individual does it by himself it becomes for him a creative act. It may result in a new piece of music, a new kind of art, a new morality or a new scientific discovery. It was achieved through a personal effort brought about by the inner urge of creative living which springs from the very essence or spirit of the human being. Any *creative* effort must function in a medium very near to the Creator, and this medium must exist in radiations much higher and finer and more potent than those of either the concrete or abstract mind. These latter can therefore be controlled and used by the 'higher' or 'creative' mind. When it acts upon or stimulates the lower mental atoms, when it brings two or more mental 'facts' or elements together and a compound is fused, heat and energy are produced by this electrified action just as in the scientist's laboratory, and intense radiation is set up.

Furthermore, when the higher mind impinges upon the atomic formation of the lower mind in order to stimulate it to a subtler activity, radioactivity is brought about whilst the coarser mental atoms are actually transmuted to their subtler and finer counterparts. This is a very important point to grasp as we have now reached the core of our subject of transmutation as it exists within the human being. Atomic energy of a very potent kind can be released within the brain of man. His essence, the will-to-be or to do, is *electrical* in character. It can therefore produce heat, stimulation and change in all the atoms in his body, similarly to the achievements of modern atomic scientists, and thereby affect the health and quality of all the bodily cells.

The seat of the creative will or mind is the pineal gland in the centre of the head. Both the pineal and the pituitary have many functions other than that of the mental. In fact we can say that the physical bodies of the glands deal with the physical functions of their host, whilst their etheric counterparts or doubles (the medium or channel for electric forces) deal with or carry the mental radiations and activities. A multiplicity of functions can thus be achieved by such an organ, especially if, as in the case of the pituitary, it is in two sections.

It is indeed wonderful to see the complexity with which the human being has built up all his functions in order to compete more successfully with the ever-increasing complexity of life itself; and in order to function in ever higher and more potent spheres of radiations, as he approaches the final and inevitable moment where, considered as an atom, he achieves transmutation and bursts his imprisoning bonds asunder altogether.

7

The human soul

THERE are two factors conditioning the human mind
which, although rather intangible, can give a far surer
clue than the somewhat confused researches into the
subconscious of traditional psychoanalysis. One is the
primeval impulse towards involution as it impinges upon
the mind. The other is the impulse towards evolution or
liberation.

We noted that the process of involution produces that
phase wherein the life becomes *involved* in physical
matter and material concerns. It is a process of concretion and crystallisation into form and habit, as
opposed to the later process of transmutation and
liberation. The Ageless Wisdom teaches that the purpose of existence on this planet so far as the human
being is concerned is the development of individual
creative power. It explains that the one Creator has
need of a constant succession of lesser Deities (Sons of
God) to aid in the running of His Universe, either as
rulers of planetary bodies or in other ways too stupendous for our embryonic minds to grasp. It is taught that
our own planet exists as a training school in which the
human being is subjected to a long process of conditioning during which the divine spark within him will
endeavour to aid the soul or conscious individuality,
firstly to develop, and secondly to orient itself to the
Divine Will and the purpose of its own existence.

The descent into matter, or involution, was designed so that the individual human spirit should know *itself* as an individual—otherwise it was conscious only of God and remained serene and static in that perfection.

So long as a drop of water is in the ocean it is conscious only of the ocean and not of itself. When it becomes separated as a drop it can have an individual life and history, it can contain its own magnetic core of electricity, it can gain and exhibit the strength necessary to hold itself together as an entity; it can contain a potentised version of all the salts of the sea; and it can reflect the whole visible world. When it returns to the ocean it carries with it an accumulation of experience and strength to contribute to the ocean.

The descent into matter of the human spirit has taken many millions of years. Its mysterious beginnings are veiled from our ken. The history that we know is only a fraction of the whole and only understood from the outer and material aspect. Vast and thrilling mysteries are awaiting discovery by a future and more adult mankind. We can at present only consider such information as has been handed down to us, and decide whether or no we will use it as a working hypothesis until such time as we can put it to the proof.

With regard to the two stages of involution and evolution, the process, according to the Ancient Wisdom, has been as follows: The human being had firstly to develop his physical body until it became a perfect instrument for his needs, and was finally almost automatically under his control. Secondly, he had to develop his emotional 'body' or vehicle, until he had organised it as a powerful instrument to act as his combustion engine, his driving force, his fiery core. Thirdly, he had to develop his concrete or 'memory' mind, by means of which he could live as a man and not as an animal.

G

Fourthly, he had to develop his abstract mind, so that it became the instrument of the Divine creative impulses received by the human conscious soul.

The soul itself is the medium which is capable of consciously reflecting the Will and the Intelligence of the Creator. Thus, in a perfected human entity his whole fully developed being becomes harmoniously attuned to the highest vibrations which impinge upon him, those which reach him through the channel of his own soul.

The involutionary period is that in which he develops body, emotions and concrete mind. It is a period of ever-increasing self-centredness. Egotism, separatism and the exploitation of others will characterise him until the moment when, having perfected the work of involution, he can become responsive to evolutionary vibration, the higher vibration of the soul which is trying to stimulate him to the conquest of and liberation from the confines of his physical, emotional and mental prisons. The stimulation of his inner core by the potent spiritual vibrations produces just the same effect as it has on the atom; a restless urge towards the unknown liberation and completeness outside. This produces increasing heat and expansion until the first destructive inner explosion occurs, which initiates radioactivity and transmutation. In man, the process is longer, subtler and more complex. So many factors are involved before the spirit-infused soul of man can take control of and remould all his parts.

During the growing period characterised by separatism and egotism, all the cells in man's body are under the mental influence, of course, and the organs which they build up are also coloured by it. Each organ will have the tendency to acquisitiveness and self-aggrandisement. Any part of man's anatomy which is a complete entity unto itself, such as the stomach, or the generative organs, is possessed of a mysterious individuality of its own, that specialised intelligence which is running and developing a function without the aid of man's deliberate participation. Such an individuality is *involutionary* by nature, seeking only its own growth, importance and pleasure. It is dependent upon its creator, man, for a higher influence. If man focuses his tendency for personal pleasure or gratification upon any of his organs, such stimulation of an egotistical kind rouses all the involutionary will to self-aggrandisement in that organ. It acquires a more and more powerful magnetic quality, and seeks to rule its creator altogether. It very often succeeds, and the man becomes a glutton, drunkard, sex-addict, or mentally obsessed in some way.

The human being, as an embryonic Deity, has to learn wise control of all his parts, giving them a fair, harmonious and equalised existence one with another. His body is like a continent of many countries; his mind is a complex of many loyalties; and his task is to produce a federation in which each member works for the good of the whole under conditions which give each part the right to complete normal fulfilment. Until he can achieve this within himself he will never achieve it outwardly, in either family life, national life or international life.

Having realised these facts, certain men throughout history have struggled with the task of 'overcoming'— that is to say of controlling and sublimating all involutionary tendencies within themselves. Often they have gone about it crudely, and sought to crush out or 'kill' out the 'Adam' within all their parts. To *suppress* a growing, developing entity of any kind only leads to frustration, resistance, poisonous by-products and abnormality. Therefore the puritanical, the tyrannical and the suppressive methods, often used individually and collectively, have only succeeded in producing abnormality and retarded development, with their innumerable complexities, of which the psychoanalysts have vainly tried to unravel and make sense.

The only way to achieve fulfilment in the human being is not to suppress anything at all, but to subject it to the highest vibration which its owner can contact or wield, that which springs from his noblest ideals, his aspiration towards an unselfish co-operation with the Creator and His Designs. Such a way of living can be acquired only through wise understanding and the steady practice of the focused will. This has been the aim of all those mysterious saints, sages, recluses, yogis and dedicated men and women of all lands who have put the approach to Divine Truth first in their lives.

When a man steadily and persistently focuses his attention on a given project he gradually collects all the life and energy within his being into a steady burning core. He becomes one-pointed instead of divided into infinite complexities. He makes of himself *one whole*, a powerful instrument sounding and radiating a certain note, a certain quality, a certain affirmation. Such a condition is assured of success. Such a project is bound to reach achievement because the human mind, when it becomes cohered into the one-pointed instrument of the will, becomes such a powerful burning-glass, channel or magnet that its influence is immeasurable. It sends out rays which reach that which it desires and, through similarity of vibration, draws the desired thing towards its own environment. It can impinge on other minds at any distance away. It can draw to itself thought-forms and patterns and ideas already suspended in the ethers. It has access to 'inspiration'; that is to say it can plug in and receive material from the Universal Intelligence and creative matrix. It can, being powerful, radiate its own quality and content in high-powered waves of influence.

There is no limit to the influence, activity and achievement possible to a man who has co-ordinated all the parts of his body, his emotions and his mind into one concentrated instrument of the will. If his will is actuated by involutionary desires he will become a 'Hitler'. If his will is actuated by evolutionary aspiration he will become a 'Gandhi'. Hitler was focused to personal power, cruelty, tyranny. Gandhi was focused to personal immolation, peaceful persuasion, the good of the many and the way of humility. The impression which Hitler made on the world will fade and pass, as does everything retrogressive. The impression which Gandhi made will grow and develop as does everything evolutionary.

Man, the embryonic Deity, has been given freewill because it brings the possibility of *choice*, and this produces individuality, creativity and action. Were there no choice humanity would remain automatic and static, bringing transmutation neither to himself nor to those other kingdoms upon which his influence impinges.

8

The mystery of spirit

In trying to explore the mysteries of life one can begin perfectly well from the 'scientific' approach or the world of tangible 'facts'. From this angle one can work through from the outer to the inner, until one arrives at the core of it all, the life-impulse itself, that which is behind and the cause of atomic energy, that to which man has given the name of Spirit.

To the materialistic mind one will appear to have changed one's horses in midstream, to have changed from the steed of scientific research to the winged horse of metaphysical speculation. But does, in fact, the study of material science from its tangible to its intangible forms bring us to any point where there is a change-over from matter to spirit? Have not the scientists themselves courageously admitted that matter and energy are synonymous, and are obviously actuated by an omniscient intelligence which works through, around and within? In what better words could the scientist describe the transcendant spirit of the Creator?

Science declares that *all* is energy; that substance is energy temporarily crystallised; and that not only can substance be reconverted into energy in the laboratory, but energy can also be reconverted into substance once more. His instruments of research allow the scientist to watch processes in action during which 'solid' particles appear and disappear in, and with, a flash!—from out

THE MYSTERY OF SPIRIT 103

of nowhere! He is practically able to watch the *creation* of the initial particles of matter from the cosmic waves. He is now faced with the 'scientific fact' that particles and units of energy are released from atoms in which, apparently, they could *not* have been contained, and that particles of substance are produced in the atmosphere spontaneously, generated without any ingredients having been there—generated, therefore, from pure vibration.

It would appear that scientists are now able to watch the actual creation of matter by an invisible and transcendent force which lies back of all the phenomena of growth and life. It is this force which we call spirit, or the will and essence of the Creator. As this force is now observable in action it cannot be denied by sceptics although they may give it any name they choose. Through their own efforts the men of science are proving the existence and activity of creative spirit.

Therefore when we now seek to define this spirit, and consider what its discovery signifies, we cannot surely be accused of being 'unscientific'? Nor, when we seek the definitions and conclusions of the greatest minds of the past on this same subject, can we allow their findings to be dismissed as unscientific or imaginative. It is surely becoming more a question of different terminology and language. There can be no reason why we should not profit by and enrich ourselves with the results of aeons of deep research into these matters by people whom we admit were the geniuses of their times.

Naturally mistakes were made, as they are made today. Of course there were charlatans, and knowledge was often prostituted. Nevertheless the core and theme of ancient knowledge is essentially the same the world over. It is that invariable core only which, in scientific research, we should seek out. We know that invariable core as the Ageless Wisdom. Vast tomes and archives have existed in many parts of the world, describing and enlarging upon its postulates. The Ageless Wisdom defines the basic aspects of the Plan of Evolution, the design of the Heavens, the part which mankind and all the kingdoms of nature play in the scheme, the invisible world of beings of all grades who are a part of the scheme, and the journey by which the human spirit descends into matter and passes through the school of experience on this earth. It explains how the process of transmutation can develop within man until he gradually breaks out of the veiling prison of matter and begins to perceive and to sense the world of realities in which his physical prison is suspended. It explains how such realisation and liberation destroy the inhibitions with which he hitherto bound and dammed up the flow of atomic energy within himself. It shows how this released flow can potentise and rejuvenate him, in conjunction with his own growing spiritual realisation, as it channels him to the universal spiritual intelligence of God.

It shows, in other words, how a human being can reach real inner adulthood, can change from an ignorant, confused would-be 'believer' into one who is getting to *know*, to see and to wish to play his part in the Divine Plan. This 'growing up', this awakening to the existence of the inner spiritual world, and, above all, this taking of responsibility for one's own development and service in the Divine Plan, has been called the 'Second Birth' in the Christian religion, and the attainment of Nirvana in the Buddhist religion. The fact that the occidental will apply it in humanitarian *outer* activity, whilst the oriental will prefer to exercise *inner* humanitarian activity, does not divide the essential fact of an inner force at work, which brings enlight-

enment, and speeds up the transmutation and radioactivity already initiated in the dedicated person.
Serenity, wisdom and many another sign will be visible
to those who know how to look.

Scientific research is, in the last analysis and at its
best, out to procure happiness, health and good living
for mankind. Spiritual research is out for the same ends.
The two factors, the inner and the outer, are converging
with great rapidity. When they meet surely something
momentous will happen—a joining of the two great
forces, the 'practical activity' with inner enlightenment.
This could produce concerted right action in the world,
a factor which has never existed before. It could bring
in a quite new era of possibilities and of eventualities.

There is, I suppose, no one who would deny the
existence of the physical body. We have developed all
our senses to concentrate upon it and upon all that we
can experience through it. There is probably no one
who would deny the world of emotions, no one who has
not been carried away by them in *spite* of a violent
mental effort to prevent it. A little thought will
convince us that the mind and the emotions can act
quite separately and in direct opposition. In fact we try
to use the mind, its arguments (record playing) and its
force (the will behind it) in order to control our emotions, which, when stimulated, seem to have a life and
a reasoning power of their own. It is not difficult to
perceive that the emotions seem to have built themselves up almost as a separate entity within us, which is
for ever trying to gain the upper hand. They appear to
strive to loosen our self-control and our sense of proportion. They try to set us on fire and to sweep us into wild
impulsive orgies of feeling, in spite of the fact that the
mind 'knows better' and is on the side of caution and
self-protectiveness. If we listen to the mind we may be

too cautious. If we obey our emotions we are not cautious enough. People have always tried to sort out these enigmas within the human consciousness. It is extraordinarily difficult and needs careful watching and a quite unprejudiced approach. If we watch ourselves in all our reactions to the happenings of the day, we may begin to learn things about ourselves that we had not suspected. What, for instance, happens when we meet a person for the first time? Our emotions react to the emotional set-up of that person, to the radiations which he sends out to us or to the world in general. Our emotions will be inclined to welcome the person if it is welcome that he desires, to echo his fear if he is afraid. Meanwhile the concrete mind gets to work playing over various records to see if they will meet the situation. Should we trust this person—is he an enemy? Is he a useful person to know? Should we take a firm hand with him? Should we speak first, apart from the automatic 'How do you do?', which means nothing, and 'It's a nice day today', which means little more?

The mind will sense if its partnering emotions are over-friendly and will try to restrain them with its own caution. There will be a battle between caution and the emotional desire for experience. Who has not felt this inner struggle? Who would seriously deny the conflict between the emotional entity within us who wants to feel and experience at all costs, and that other mental entity within us who is always out for self-protection, and who tries to achieve it by playing over all his 'cautious' records? We can know and recognise these two entities within us, the one who uses only unreasoning feelings, and the other who uses well-used words.

But there is a third entity within us who uses neither arguments nor feelings, but who quickly and deliberately, in one second, faces and states the true situation.

We sometimes call this entity the 'still small voice'. It is a part of us that really *knows*. We believe that it is a super-conscious part of ourselves, and we sometimes call it our 'conscience' and sometimes our 'soul'. We declare that it is superconscious because we realise that it is above our normal thinking, and that it is not influenced by emotions nor by mental arguments. It remains definite and instantaneous in its affirmation. Both the emotions and the mentality are aware that the 'still small voice' is *always* right, that it is indeed superior to themselves. Nearly always they try to deafen themselves to it with their own vibrational clamour. Often they succeed. Nevertheless it lies behind all the grosser, noisier preoccupations, a sure and certain anchor at which the emotions could calmly ride, a steady beacon to direct the mind. It is the inner link with the Universal Intelligence, the mysterious channel to wisdom which is the birthright of every normal human being.

We have therefore several conflicts which are taking place within ourselves most of the time. There is the conflict between the desires of the emotions and those of the mind. There is the conflict between each of these and the superconscious or soul, that which knows and proclaims right action. Besides this there is the conflict between what the person in question wishes to do or think, and the pressures exerted upon him by one or more people or circumstances with which he is connected. There are in fact the countless adjustments which he has to make in all his personal relationships.

The point is that *each* of these conflicts and adjustments *uses up energy* and divides the mental instrument within itself. Actually, the perpetual mental arguments, mental muscular restrictions or inhibitions, which are brought into play in this complex situation, use up a quite vast amount of electrical energy. This energy is *atomic energy*, constantly drained from the subtle atoms who channel it and the cells who are trying to store it. If we did not tamper with it by squandering it on all our inner conflicts, it would represent an enormous bank balance of potent power at our disposal. If we were to keep it intact we would be possessed of superhuman reserve force which would express itself as radiant health and abundant self-expression. If this inner reserve force was husbanded instead of squandered it would bank up as a fiery core within us, resulting in radioactivity.

It would seem, therefore, that the great need is to find out the way to resolve our inner conflicts. We could also try to imagine what would be the results of the ensuing radioactivity, were we able to do so.

Scientists have been able to detect and measure the radiations from the brain. One American scientist, Ruth Drown, invented a mechanism by means of which she photographed the electrical workings of both the mind and body, using only the light emitted by the inner bodily electricity. (These photographic slides have been seen by the author.)

We know that in order to contract and move one of our muscles we have to send an electrical message or spark along the nerve to the muscle-ending. Arrived there it burns up the sugar stored there to produce the energy for the movement (a chemical change always produces energy). Even a little study will prove to us that every breath, movement and thought uses up energy. But thought itself, whose medium is of a higher finer vibration, uses up the energy from the more subtilised cells and atoms within the body, and, as we have observed, these are by far the most powerful and can control and affect all the rest.

Because of all those conflicts *perpetually* at work within ourselves, sleeping or waking, we suffer from a tremendous loss of energy. Our human battery is drained constantly and in every direction. We are therefore, although potentially 100 horse-power, as it were, only able to function on five horse-power! The rest of our receiving apparatus is corroded or empty or out of function. This results in many deficiency conditions or strain, or stresses which we know as disease.

It follows that in order to build up and restore our own potential, the first requisite is to resolve our inner conflicts. We must find out how to overcome the rival attitudes of our emotions, our minds and our superconscious. One of these three must be put in control and the others aligned with it. This is not really an impossible or complicated process, but it does need *understanding*. For aeons men have striven to perform this feat, as they have always known that thereby was the way to fulfilment and their heritage of divinity. I am of course referring to the intelligentsia and esotericists of every age in history.

They usually, however, made certain grave mistakes. We know well the tradition in religious instruction which urges us to *kill* the desire within us, to repress all our 'sinful' instincts, to deny ourselves indulgence. All these injunctions would, if followed, cause us to dam up the electrical impulses within us and the swirling astral atoms impelled by the will, so that they all turn in upon themselves and are short-circuited. Desire is not killed, it is inhibited, betrayed, choked and frustrated. Great harm is done. It is senseless to try to do away with desire, which is the movement of the emotions. Desire is the fountain-head of action, the fire of living. It is the instrument which the soul uses to convey the urge to live, to be and to experience. Without it all would be cold, mechanical and static.

The mind is the instrument which assimilates the

experiences initiated by impulse—desire. Without the mind, the memory and *results* of experience would be lost. Without the emotions there could be no experience, no real growth. Both are the essential tools of the soul. The soul is a medium between the mind and emotions (the lower vibrations) and the Universal Divine Intelligence or the spirit (the highest vibrations). The soul is the intermediary, the subtle linking sheath between spirit and bodily living. It is a kind of reflector, reflecting the will and the Plan of Divine Intelligence from above (highest vibrations) and the essence of experience from the instruments below (mind and emotions). The reflection from above (the will of God, or Good, or evolution) we know as the 'still small voice'. It is instantaneous in action because it is the reflection of wordless 'truth'. It proclaims the nature of 'good or evil' according to its place on the involutionary or evolutionary ladder. It perceives instantly what a thing is.

In considering the subtle gradation of atoms from the coarsest and most 'solid' to the finest of all, the 'atoms' of the soul, the latter are those next in degree to the spiritual essence itself—the instigator of all life. From the soul the divine impulse is reflected to the mental atoms of the abstract mind, and these are able, if conditions are sufficiently harmonious, to step it down to the lower vibration of the atoms of the concrete mind, where it is translated into conceptions, thoughts and *words*. This takes place through the medium of, firstly, the pineal gland, which can receive the impression of wordless spiritual concepts.

In order to step the latter down into words and actually workable thoughts, the pituitary body must be brought into action. The frontal lobe receives and interprets the ideal or abstract concepts, whilst the posterior lobe translates them into the pattern of resulting activities. We can see from this the necessity for co-operation between these glands. However, as the pineal is the highest instrument of the mental processes, and the pituitary of the emotional processes, if there is conflict between the emotional desires and the mental aims, no proper co-operation is possible, and, as in the majority of cases, divine truths and the divine impulse to right action cannot be passed on from pineal to pituitary, and cannot be apprehended by the thinking brain.

Here we have the crux of the whole question of human development. We have the reason for the religions and esoteric practices of all time. In all the major schools of spiritual teaching, whether they are orthodox religious bodies or esoteric groups, the teaching is divided into degrees or sections. At first there is the outer teaching for the general public. Then comes an amplification for the serious student. Later he can qualify himself for the beginnings of the inner esoteric studies. By this time his mind is able to grasp, and worthy to be trusted with, secrets of living which would be entirely incomprehensible to and unsuitable for the general public. In other words, his training is producing within himself a process of transmutation of the mental atoms. They have been changing from the coarser atoms of the lower vibrational concrete mind to finer and finer atoms with higher and more powerful vibratory rates for use by the abstract mind, and finally by the channels of spiritual reception. Whilst the mental atoms are thus changed and refined they build subtler and finer physical atoms and cells within the brain, capable of receiving the impressions of spiritual and universal truth.

When we speak of *truth* we refer to those many spiritual and cosmic laws by which the universe is built

and run and by which the process of evolution is en-
sured. These laws have been indicated in the Ageless
Wisdom and are well known to esoteric students. An
assessment of their validity and their relationship with
modern scientific findings can easily be made by
personal and independent study, which gives the only
sound criterion.* Many people are aspiring to break
out of their prison of self-centred crystallised thought
patterns. They are seeking to know God, His Works and
His Plan, in order to live accordingly and serve humanity to some purpose. Such people are constantly
reaching for, and orienting their minds towards, their
mirror of truth, the soul. They are ready to listen to the
'still small voice'. In order to do so they must hush the
clamour of the coarser, louder vibrations within their
beings. They must resolve all their inner conflicts and
bring peace and stillness within.

When the emotions have ceased to flurry and swirl
and demand; when the mind has ceased to play its
interminable records, sometimes several at the same
time; and when the demands and self-importance of
many of the bodily organs have been calmed down—
then at last a great hush spreads throughout the
personality. The energies no longer drain rapidly away,
the human battery no longer works overtime. The
emotions and the mind are *still*, which is a wonderful
and almost terrifying new experience. They are still
as a lake, as reflecting water. In fact they become as a
reflection to that world of truth which is seen by the
soul. Truth can then pass straight through into human
realisation as if it were passing through several panes
of clear glass. Things are instantly seen as *they are*; right
action is instinctive; problems are seen in their clarifica-
tion; the Divine Will and the goal ahead are glimpsed.

* See *Initiation of the World* by the author.

The human being has, for perhaps a few seconds, broken through his prison into the world of life and truth which surrounds him and in fact permeates him. Wireless instrument that he is, he has been able for a brief moment to plug in to the highest (and most silent) stratum of life: that which lies behind and within, that which we call the eternal. For one moment the student has achieved unity with the source of life. This unity has been the goal of all more profound schools of human-spiritual development. One of the oldest of all these sciences is the historic Asiatic training which we know as Yoga. Yoga means 'union'. It is the science which strives to harmonise and unite all the warring parts of man, physical, mental and emotional, to put them finally under the dominance of spirit, the Will of the Creator, which exists within all His created beings.

As man aspires and trains towards such a goal, the goal, in fact, of his divine heritage, he puts into action the process of transmutation within himself. As he learns to lose interest in materialistic or sensual thoughts, their coarser atoms and brain cells disintegrate through disuse. They are transmuted and refined in the use of the higher grades of thought which supersede. The total vibrational note of the personality changes and its effect on every atom and cell in the body is very potent. All is gradually resolved into a harmonious orchestra under one vibrationary leadership, and with constant steady radioactivity. This radioactivity takes place as the heavy static atoms, which form the imprisoning chrysalis of thought habits around the perceptions, are stimulated and heated by the emotions of aspiration until they disintegrate. Thus the atoms of materialistic thought have been split by the soul, or by the one-pointed fire of the dedicated mind under its influence.

H

From the womb of materialism, the womb of matter, the 'second birth' is about to take place.

This 'second birth' brings forth a new type of human being. He is no longer an embryonic creature, tightly entombed in thoughts not of his own making. He is an adult aspiring soul, having taken responsibility for his own existence, his own knowledge, his own progress and his own part in the Divine Plan. He is free from self-imprisonment. He is selfless. He is dedicated to learn the Divine Purpose and to live it completely and actively. He belongs now to a new and quite different species of humanity—he is definitely a 'God in the making'. His way of living and thinking would be incomprehensible to the 'average man' he once was. His only emotion is that of love. But it is not a personal love. It is that embracing radiance of God in which he now takes part —a love for all creation at all its different stages—a love made possible by the wisdom of one who knows a little of the Plan, and sees all striving creatures in their relationship to it.

Such is the picture of the transmutation of the human being. Such is the way in which he splits his own mental atoms through the heat of the emotions and the electrical currents of the mind, under the impress of the evolutionary impulse coming through the soul. It is as much a scientific portrayal as any other. It deals with the inner force at work within all life, with atoms, with electricity, with the processes of disintegration, radio-activity, transmutation into subtler atoms; with the resolving of matter in human form into its highest essences.

There is, however, a difference. The laboratory processes are exploratory, uncertain, artificial and in many respects contrary to natural processes. They may end destructively through ignoring evolutionary laws. The transmutation which takes place in a human being can only follow the law. It can only produce sublimation of all the atoms which come within its ring-pass-not. It can only send out radiations of an ever more subtilised potency. Its effects are towards the liberation and spiritualisation of all the kingdoms in nature which it touches. It works under the laws of nature, in natural scientific fashion for the liberation and fulfilment of all life on this earth.

9

The essence of all life

I F we try to reach to the inner core and source of all life, how far can we expect to go?

The electrical fires and radiations set free by the atomic scientists are so fierce that they must not be contacted by human flesh. The energies and radiations freed in atomic explosions are so poisonous and corrosive that they eat through into the very bones, bringing about diseases never known before.

It could be anticipated that a further breaking down of the atom, the vehicle of life, if that becomes possible, may release forces of even greater destructiveness and burning power. What, then, is the nature of the ultimate force or fire within the innermost core of life? Is it a destructive element and a burning power more fierce than any of its outer sheaths, or could it be something of an entirely different nature?

We only experience heat and light from the sun's rays because of their friction upon the atoms and molecular particles in the atmosphere, and because of their reflection from the crystalline surfaces of these particles. Heat is the result of friction, change and movement. If there were spaces in the universe where no friction, change and movement exist, we should expect to find neither light nor heat. If, therefore, we were able to remove all the physical sheaths from an atom until we reached its innermost life essence, there would then be nothing to produce heat or fire, therefore, apparently, nothing destructive. There could only be that living potent urge which had brought the atom into being—that urge which is present throughout space, which is the ultimate will of the Creator, and which we call SPIRIT.

In breaking through ever nearer to the essence of the atom, the scientists are making an approach to God Himself. They are stripping off the robe of God, physical matter, in a more intimate way than ever before. That which they might ultimately set free may not burn or destroy in the physical sense, but its impact would have far more powerful effects in another way. Such radiations might affect those grades of radiations in their environment which are most nearly allied to them. They would therefore affect most powerfully the innermost core of man himself—his own spiritual essence, his own *raison d'être*.

When Moses 'saw God' he was struck down. When the disciples saw Christ conversing with Elijah they fell to the ground, 'blinded'. Whatever the truth of these stories, they certainly indicate what would, in fact, happen if naked spiritual radiance should be contacted by a human being. The impact of a high and transmuted spiritual embodiment, although it would neither burn nor shine in the physical sense, would certainly exert a terrific vibrational impact which would stimulate the lesser and feebler soul of man more greatly than could be borne. Such a mighty stimulation could shatter man's own sheaths, and could cause, if not death, a loss of consciousness.

Throughout history it has always been stated that people who had attained to great spirituality were seen to have a halo or nimbus around their heads, described as an aura of light, either white, gold or of many delicate colours. We have probably never thought much about the *meaning* of this phenomenon, vouched for and represented in paintings and sculptures all over the world. Now, however, that we are learning the facts of radioactivity, it is becoming possible to understand the mystery of the proverbial halo demonstrated by all the greatest of historical saints. It is simply radioactivity in its ultimate and highest form, when it is perfected within a human being. The aura of such a saint or sage is so potent that its high vibrations can catalyse the atoms of and effect changes within all bodies of lower vibration which they contact. It is in this way that physical healing and mental regeneration can be brought about. In performing an act of healing the co-ordinated and spiritually controlled mind can direct the radiations of its own aura, concentrating them and projecting them towards the place where the need is. Naturally, if the sufferer himself is able to tune in his own receiving apparatus to the incoming vibrations by an act of 'faith' or comprehending will, the results will be more assured. 'According to thy faith be it done unto thee!' Even with men of only moderate spiritual development, if conditions are favourable, such healing work can be and often is accomplished.

The aura of a saint is the expression of that condition wherein the physical atoms have become so finely transmuted that they are able to hold, reflect and express the spiritual radiations themselves, without there being any longer a veil or successive veils of coarser physical atoms intervening. Spirit and matter, at its finest, have become one. The complete unity achieved between the mental, emotional and physical atoms has enabled this fusion to take place. The man is now a spirit in action. The power of uninhibited atomic energy is his. The channel through to all-knowledge and all-wisdom is his. The capacity to

project his thought around the world and throughout
eternity is his also. He is the fulfilled man—the emerging Son of God, the Twice-Born.

Have there ever been any men like this? History
indicates a few perfect examples and many of lesser perfection. In fact history can show us a long ladder of
successive grades of such achieving souls, ranging from
very imperfect men with yet the divine spark of genius
working through them, right up to the rare examples of
the ultimate achievement.

The story of Jesus Christ shows us a good picture of
the perfect man. The mysteries of His miracles, healings,
resurrection and transfiguration are all descriptions of
radioactivity at its highest expression. A body composed
of the finest radioactive atoms could not actually die,
for such atoms are already free from the laws of physical
disintegration. A man with such a body could deliberately concretise it into molecular physical solidity for
the purpose of conscious contact with average human
beings. This is known as 'materialisation'. Lesser forms
of it are believed to be enacted at the present time by
certain of the spiritualist mediums or practitioners. It
is a phenomenon which awaits future scientific 'discovery', and also the conditions afforded by a future and
more refined way of living. But it has always existed as
one of the secret laws of nature.

A second example of a spiritualised life is that of
Gautama the Buddha. For many years he subjected
himself to rigorous hardships, discipline and suffering in
the endeavour to refine and transmute the atoms of his
being to the point where he could apprehend and absorb
truth. He sought the aid of the sages, recluses or yogis
who were trying to achieve sublimation through suffering, by starving themselves, lying on beds of nails,
holding their arms permanently in the air, and by other

means practised in the orient for thousands of years. It has always been believed that the act of bearing pain and privation necessitates the binding together of the emotional and mental sensibilities under a one-pointed and steady control, producing the situation, as we have described it, in which the soul can reflect all-knowledge through into the physical brain. Therefore, throughout history hundreds of oriental *sadhus* and occidental monks have received various degrees of illumination through the practice of pain and privation. This is a thought which could well be borne in mind by those people who today have to bear suffering. It *could* be turned to very good account.

The Buddha however rejected such self-imposed hardships. He seated Himself under the famous Bod (fig) tree, deciding that He would neither move from there nor take any nourishment until He received the ultimate illumination. Thus, through a *complete* surrender of His whole being, He finally achieved sublimation. His being was refined and transmuted to the point where there was nothing between Himself and the Divine spirit of creation, the Universal Intelligence. His consciousness functioned in the world of the 'still small voice' in the sphere of wordless knowing. Through the 'second birth' He had become the perfected and complete man. It was very difficult to put into words that which He had found, as it always must be, so that even a fraction of it could be understood by the average aspiring man. His teachings about 'Nirvana', the state of illumination, have been misinterpreted and distorted by frail mankind, just as have all other great spiritual pronouncements. Yet the inner core of the thought which He projected bore its own powerful vibrational note, which has kept it in being as a concept of truth anchored on earth, so that it has persisted throughout all the involutionary and evolutionary changes of oriental history.

The same applies in even greater fashion to the teaching of Christ. Moreover, He said to mankind, 'Lo, I am with you always!' Here we have a mystery to which our present studies might give us a clue. For, since science and esotericism have almost reached a meeting-point, it is not irreverent to seek spiritual truths through the door of scientific thought, and vice versa.

We can perhaps already begin to understand that the atoms of the body of Christ were so transmuted that they were really etheric atoms, atoms of the four ethers. He could, by an act of the will, congeal these atoms into physical or solid molecules, so that He possessed an apparently normal body with which to function among men and be apprehended by them. Through the medium of this body He was able to anchor in the memory of mankind His perfected personality and His teachings. Through His embodiment in etheric atoms He was enabled after His physical 'death' to remain thereafter permanently in touch with mankind through the medium of the ethers. It is only man's chrysalis of materialistic thought which insulates him from perception of the ethers and of all that he could contact therein. Under the impact of all the stimulating pressure which his own endeavours are bringing to bear upon him, he is becoming ever more subtilised, highly strung and perceptive. It would seem that he will finally reach the point where his chrysalis wears so thin that he begins to perceive through it the world of inner realities.

This chrysalis needs careful visualising. It does not cut man off from any outer world, but from the 'Heaven within', from the channel to truth* and power which lies deep within his being and which can plug in his

* Known as the Antahkarana.

consciousness to the stratum of life which is in fact permeating him all the time. Just as the power of the atom is locked and bound within its physical particles, and seeks liberation from within in order to transcend physical matter, so it is with man. That illumination and liberation which he seeks lies *within* his own atoms and cells. What he has to break through is an electrical concretisation built by the concrete mind. In average mankind this process takes place over hundreds of thousands of years. But when once a man has summoned his will to the task of achieving liberty and illumination, he can, through one-pointed concentration of the electrical fires of his mind, burn up the dross and debris of accumulated-thought habits, speeding up the process so rapidly that instead of wearing thin, his chrysalis may crack and burst open. This dangerous event would fling him naked into the world of truth, and would represent an olympic and terrible feat of strength. His physical body or his concrete mind may not be able to support it. Such an endeavour was referred to in the Bible as 'taking the Kingdom of Heaven by storm'.

If, however, with care, understanding and devotion, a man perseveres with the purifying of all his bodily and mental atoms, his consciousness will eventually begin to function in the etheric strata. If his being and his aspirations are oriented towards the Christ Who is with us always, he will be in a position, as a perfected wireless instrument, to align himself, if such a thing is possible, with those greatest of all vibrations.

10

Our personal relation to the atom

THE atom was the first product of creation. It was the initial concretion of the Divine Breath. It was the form which the Word of Divine vibration first impressed upon the ether. It was the little seed of life itself, the embryo which held all the possibilities and patterns of creation. It was also a little swirling vortex through which is channelled the pure energy of the Creator and the impress or impulse of His purpose.

The gateway to 'Heaven', or the sphere of creation and of ultimate reality, lies within the atom; not the atom of the atomic scientist, which is really a large molecule containing an infinite number of the real atoms and their subsidiary particles. Now, in order to bind these millions of cosmic atoms of infinite variety together within the structure of one 'molecular' atom (scientists' atom) of physical matter, an enormous compression of energy is required, a prodigious binding power. In order further to bind the molecular atoms together to form the physical molecule of an element or compound, still more energy must be compressed. To build a great number of neutrons into the nuclei of the more heavy of radioactive minerals uses up still more energy. It is this agglomeration of three degrees of energy which is attacked and partly broken up by the atomic scientist.

We know that the laboratory atom links with others

of its own kind or another kind, to form molecules of an element, or basic single substance, or else of a compound. Such a molecule, if solid, takes the form of a minute crystal. A crystal is a perfect symmetrical shape, one of those archetypal patterns suspended in the ether, built there by converging lines of force which come from outer space. An atom of iron, however (since metals do not form molecules), congeals when taking solid shape around that mould or framework in the ether which belongs to its own wave-length and vibration.

It becomes a minute hard crystal, the smallest possible particle of the element, iron. A quantity of such crystals will then link together to form greater crystals along the same design, and these packed crystals will eventually form a piece of recognisable iron.

Under varying conditions of atmosphere or pressure, the atoms within an element so formed may combine with the atoms of other elements to become compounds —that is to say substances with quite a different character to their component elements; or they may link loosely with other elements to form mixtures in which their individual characters are not lost. In a piece of coal, for instance, one will discover both compounds and mixtures. In the atmosphere also there are both compounds and mixtures.

We have seen that the making of ever more subtle compounds results in the formation of living organic tissues, either of plant, animal or man. We have seen that the coarse mineral molecule in the soil is digested or split up by the acid secretions of the tiny bacteria into particles small enough to make them soluble in water. In that form minerals can be taken up by the plant and refined and built up into compounds which are assimilable by man and the rest of the animal kingdom.

The human being also uses acids to split up many of the substances which he eats. The cells of his digestive glands are so marvellous that they can design and produce a digestive juice for each kind of food which he chooses to consume. An acid is a positive, masculine, active substance. In excess it is corrosive, destructive, over-active and quarrelsome. An alkali is a negative, feminine, peaceful substance, engaged in storing energy. In excess it is lethargic and chilling. All the tissues and all the workings of the human body are built and run on the basis of the right proportions of acid and alkali, just as is any other electric battery. In the muscles, which engage in activity, we find the acid. In the blood, which holds the life, we find the alkaline condition. It follows that any thought or emotion which stimulates to strain, tension or action produces extra acid. But the balance between acid and alkali in a body must be kept in the right proportions to ensure good health. The wild animal knows exactly what to eat, when to eat and how much to eat, in order to keep its metabolism correctly balanced. But our degenerated human has forgotten everything about this essential knowledge. Usually he would even deny its importance. He eats an appalling mixture of wrongly balanced foods, in which the acid usually completely outweighs if not altogether swamps the alkali. The result is that he is continually suffering from acidity. Acidity irritates the nervous system, producing a strongly quarrelsome, critical and pugnacious temperament. This, of course, results in more tensions, strains and activities, thus producing still further acidity. The excess acid floods the blood-stream, seeps into the bony structure, clogs the nerves. We suffer from a host of elaborately named 'diseases' which are simply the results of excess acid, nothing more. The acid also breaks into the very cells of the body, invading the alkaline 'sea' in which the chromosome electric battery is insulated and at work storing the energies of the cosmic rays. The acid invades and short-circuits this arrangement. It corrodes the chromosome filaments. The cell can no longer function. It is cut off from the cosmic rays, its source of power, character and stimulation. When this condition engulfs many of the bodily cells the results are naturally catastrophic. The cells lose their ring-pass-not, their radiation which protected them and kept the balance between their own work and that of the many bacteria and microbes who do their particular work in the blood-stream. These microbes, hitherto beneficial, now begin to feast on the dying cells, and multiply to the point where they gain the upper hand. We call this condition an infectious disease.

People vary enormously, according to their individual orientation towards the various glands of the body and of the cosmic rays back of them. Human beings come under many classifications in this respect. Whichever gland dominates the body, the latter will assume formation, characteristic and qualities accordingly. A gland specialist, when looking at a patient, can usually tell at once whether he is an 'adrenal type', or a 'pituitary type'. He can also say whether his patient is 'hyper-pituitary' or 'hypo-pituitary', or in other words whether he suffers from over-activity or deficiency in that gland. The very formation and size of the bones, the teeth, the hair and the colouring are all indicative of the person's state of glandular development. As for the mental and emotional side, this too is strongly affected by the state of the glands. As most of us have heard, it is often possible to cure imbecility by a glandular operation. Giantism or dwarfism is also due to glandular abnormality.

Why do the glands have such a vital influence upon

the whole make-up of the individual? The answer is
not far to seek. We have mentioned that there are seven
major glands in the body, and that they are built
around an invisible core of energy which is the channel
for certain planetary rays. In fact these cores, or
'centres' as they are called, represent the solar system
of the body. Each centre controls a gland, and each
gland builds one of the organs of the body, and each
of these organs depends upon the mineral which
'belongs' to the planet in question. This interesting
science has been studied as an aspect of astrology. But
it is also closely connected with other modern sciences,
such as Biochemistry. With its aid much successful
healing work is done.

Our own purpose, however, is to indicate how
closely interwoven are the physical tissues with the
mind, the emotions, the minerals which build them,
and the cosmic rays which initiate their activities. We
want to emphasise the fact that, as the scientist states,
all is energy; and substance, which is but congealed
energy, is interchangeable into energy, and vice versa.

If we accept the picture which we have presented, of
life being built up by means of a long scale of graded
atoms, from the gross molecular atom of the laboratory,
through to the finer transmuted atoms some of which
ultimately change into etheric atoms, then transmute
further into astral or emotional atoms, and finally
become mental atoms, we shall understand more easily
the way in which the interchange of energy into substance takes place within the human body. We shall
understand the way in which a state of mind can
impinge upon all the atoms and cells within the body
and produce chemical changes of a radical nature.

If we think in a combative, critical or envious way,
we will not only produce acidity in the body, but we will

set up the vibration of *greed* within the personality. This greed, whether it expresses itself in ambition, or gluttony, or possessiveness, will generate acidity to a remarkable degree. It will also predispose its owner to consume and use all the more acid-forming of foods, and indulge in the more acid of occupations. A vicious circle will be set up. Because of the indulgence in an egotistical or greedy thought, the impulse for exploitation is encouraged. The personality is oriented to the habit of *using* others. He becomes a 'taker', perhaps a parasite. Whereas an orientation in the other extreme, an uncritical, easy-going, and generous attitude, will produce an alkaline nature, the one who is exploited, a 'giver'. This, if carried to excess, also has its drawbacks, as we must often have noticed.

In the normal way every living creature should be both a giver and a taker. These functions should be active on all planes, that is to say physically and psychically. From the physical and electrical angle, each kingdom of nature gives something to the kingdom below it and to the kingdom above it, and takes something from each. This complete interdependence and interaction ensure that long chain of transmutation which we call evolution. Any creature which takes without giving, we call a parasite. Many parasites do, in fact, serve some useful purpose. A few are destructive only. We find examples in the plant world, the insect and the animal world. A remarkable fact about them is that, when compared with the 'givers', the 'takers' never flourish. Their numbers always remain a small fraction of those of the givers; their lives are shorter; their emanations are less wholesome; they seem less capable of either learning anything or of further evolution. In the plant world we can think of the ivy and the mistletoe in this connection. Amongst animal life we can note the vermin, leeches and worm parasites.

We can, in fact, include carnivorous animals under this heading. They certainly conform to our list of characteristics. Their numbers never become great. They are difficult to 'tame' or teach; their flesh is unpleasant as food; their emanations and aromas are harmful. At the bottom of this list come the vultures and other scavengers, those who feed upon corpses, even putrefying corpses. They, be it noted, are the most unwholesome creatures of all.

The vegetarian animals, by comparison, are more numerous, long-lived, patient, teachable and adaptable. They are rather 'alkaline' in their nature. Their drawback is that they have to spend so many of the hours of daily life in feeding, heads downwards, in order to obtain their needed sustenance from green food. Such a life is not conducive to the development of intelligence. At the top of this list, however, we find the fruitarian animals, the apes and gorillas. Fruit and nuts are a complete and highly concentrated food, needing but little digestion, and producing no waste matter in the body. Therefore the fruitarian animals spend but little time eating. They are highly intelligent, full of fun and pranks and very teachable. The gorilla is actually the strongest creature in the jungle, whom, apparently, no other beast can tackle.

We know, of course, of the strong kinship which man has with these fruitarian species. His teeth, intestines, and many other features proclaim him to be a fruitarian by origin and by nature. For many thousands of years he has betrayed the designs of the Creator, and broken down his own bodily and mental health and vigour, through gluttony and degraded feeding. He has prostituted himself to the degree that he cannot even be

I

considered as a carnivore but more as a scavenger, an eater even of corpses which have become 'high' or putrid. Through his desire for flesh-eating he has upset the whole economy of nature, through the breeding and herding of millions of animals he has caused widespread soil erosion, disease in soil, plant, animal and in himself. Moreover, through this terrible betrayal of the Divine Plan (the true 'Fall of Man'), his spiritual development has been stultified and arrested, and therefore also his essential intelligence. It has caused him constantly to flood the planet with emanations of greed, exploitation and callous blood-thirstiness. On these emanations the whole of the animal kingdom has been obliged to draw its emotional and mental sustenance for thousands of years.

No crimes against animals, no tortures, nor outrages, nor abnormalities, have been too great for man in his greed and opportunism to inflict against those weaker than himself. Such habits have developed in mankind the capacity to treat each other in the same ways, the willingness to commit the obscenity of warfare, and the stupidity which prevents them from finding other means for achieving international adjustment.

All this is being realised by many hundreds all over the world today. The number of groups and societies forming everywhere in an effort to promote peace, and every other humanitarian objective, is truly amazing. Goodwill, the wish to learn and to take the initiative in leading a better life, is growing so widespread that one can begin to anticipate that finally it may hold sway through sheer force of numbers and unity of purpose. Of course there is a long way to go yet. At present, in the contest between worldliness and the martial spirit (the 'takers') and the newer emphasis on giving and sharing and co-operating under the principle of peace, the latter is reaching the exciting stage when it may balance the scales. At that vital period the issue will depend on just how many people have given sufficient thought to the essential destiny and function of mankind as suggested in this book. Such people, by the *power of right thinking alone,* could swing down the balance in favour of regeneration and true progress, and an orientation to evolutionary values. Upon them might depend the whole future of civilisation and world history. The physical discovery of atomic energy is making clear the secret of the inner power on which mankind could learn to depend, instead of on greed and unnatural parasitism towards all the kingdoms of nature, including his own.

This situation is urgent, dramatic, in fact romantic enough to stir those of us who will face up to it and study it, to our very depths. It is, of course, nothing new. The great ones of all ages in history have been inspired by it, and have tried to speak it forth. Their words still exist for those who seek. Anyone who takes up the challenge, and attempts to regenerate himself and live the kind of life which in its aggregate would save the world, need not feel that he is being peculiar, or Utopian. He should realise that he is *in the right,* and that back of him is the power, the example and the pioneer work of very many of the greatest people in history. This may seem an astonishing statement to many of us. But the fact is that, just as some of today's press panders to the lower demands of the public, so throughout history only the more sensational aspects of the lives of the great were put before a willing public, whilst, often, their real message was pushed conveniently into the background.

A genius such as Pythagoras, Wagner or Tolstoy, nearly always has glimpses of the truth, and a realisation of the true destiny of man, and of how he should live his life, no matter how piecemeal such realisation and the achievements of his own character may be. Humanity, alas, usually seizes avidly upon the more unworthy and frail aspects of its geniuses, because emphasis upon these will help it to salve its own conscience. The same treatment will probably be meted out to the message of such men as Schweitzer later on. All such enlightened men become fired with the desire to inspire humanity to escape from their materialistic imprisonment and live the free and emancipated life of harmlessness and constructive guardianship towards all created life.

The process of self-purification, upon which all spiritual and regenerative teaching has always been based, leads to the release and use of the personal and individual atomic energy. Through the practice of a pure life, that is to say a 'whole' or complete life, unadulterated by corrosives either physically, emotionally or mentally, the debris of the old life is gradually eliminated from the system; the corrosive acids leave the cells of the body, allowing them to resume their potency; the channels to the cosmic rays are reopened; the reflection of the soul, the mirror of the inner world, is made clear; and the unlimited power of atomic energy can be tapped through all the glandular centres.

After such a wonderful development has been achieved, the person has become a walking dynamo, a permanent channel of inspiration, a potent source of radiation to all who can receive; that is to say who, no matter how imperfectly, are oriented in some measure towards the higher aspects of living. We all have the potential within us of becoming such walking dynamos. This would mean that we would become radioactive. It would mean that we have learnt to live, act and think in such a way that there is no disharmony and no crosscurrent within us, that all the factors of mind, emotions and actions are resolved as one whole organism, not divided amongst themselves, but united in strength under the will of the soul. It would mean, therefore, no diffusion or loss of energy. This alone would transform us into quite different beings, power houses of reserved force which would be transmuting all the cells of our bodies to an ever clearer, cleaner and higher potency.

We could use these new tremendous reserves of power in a variety of ways. We could turn ourselves into transmitters of spiritual thought and desire through the ethers; in which case our influence for good would be incalculable. We could use ourselves as examples to others of the good life, showing that strength, health and mental vitality can be retained until death at any age. We could further go, and demonstrate, as many saints and yogis have done, that a true 'son of God', or one who has learned to be nourished by God through the cosmic rays, is insulated from sensitivity to great heat or cold, is independent of the usual food and drink requirements, can resist poison, burning, cutting, or other injury. These faculties have been demonstrated, as we know, and considered as 'miracles' or abnormal occurrences without any 'scientific' bases.

On the contrary, our studies will have allowed us to see that they are the truly normal and scientific demonstrations of inherent human capacities and qualifications, and that these would be the natural outcome of constructive spiritually based living.

PART TWO

11

Setting ourselves free

KRISHNAMURTI has said that the true human being has not yet appeared on this earth (the human being who is functioning as a spiritually inspired dynamo, responsible to himself for instantaneous right action in all circumstances, without the interference of the resistant, insulating and separative concrete mind, packed as it is with outside influences). Such human beings, who would exploit nothing and demand nothing for the self; who would share everything and serve all without distinction; whose every thought and radiation would be constructive and helpful, would revolutionise the world's way of living as soon as their numbers had reached the necessary fraction of the world's population which would allow their collective mind-power to swing down the balance.

They would also reorient the consciousness of the animal kingdom. They would provide the consciousness of the planet with the dynamic co-operation of constructive mental units, and thus affect the whole climatic temperament, producing over the earth an atmosphere of joy, serenity and bountiful growth.

We can indeed imagine that such developments could and would transform the world into a Heaven on earth, a second Garden of Eden. Such would be the result of developing ourselves as we were meant by nature to develop. It would be the direct result of understanding the secret of atomic energy as it applies to ourselves. It would make us largely independent of a great deal of the artificial aspects of the industrial age which so enslave us at this time, aspects which could be carried forward into the Atomic Age and keep us equally bound, unless we see the way of escape.

All this may sound far-fetched, Utopian and impossible of achievement. Yet surely it is the only way towards a whole, healthy and evolutionary world civilisation? No matter what we may achieve materially and scientifically, we could still continue to reap only more difficulties, and slavery to economic drudgery, disease and war, unless and until we learn how to base our lives on spiritual and natural laws and principles. At the present time our world is seething with unrest and conflict. It is teeming with refugees and victims of both warfare and colour prejudice. Masses of the population everywhere are still undernourished and diseased. The money which should be spent on raising the level of living is squandered on armament manufacture. Cruelty, aggression and oppression are still rife. It is natural for an observer to take a disillusioned view of humanity, and fail to perceive any radical progress.

Yet, not long ago, the world everywhere was in an uproar because Britain was supposed to be committing an act of aggression against Egypt. In Britain herself the voices were raised most strongly, including even a protest signed by 100 journalists. A few generations back such a situation would have seemed impossible and quite incredible. Warfare was considered right, glorious and natural. Aggression was the normal function of all growing nations. Even individually, fighting was the normal exercise and pastime of any healthy man of good degree. Until recently duelling, on the slightest pretext, was the habitual and necessary expression of manliness.

Even the wholesale stealing of peoples from their own lands, to sell into slavery, was not considered a dishonourable activity. In fact England publicly declared that her interests and her economics could not suffer the abolishment of slavery.

Yet recently a large proportion of the British public was horribly ashamed because Britain was trying to separate two small combating countries by means of what she carefully called 'police intervention'!—whilst horror and condemnation of this act was being declaimed all over the world. Why cannot we realise what a wonderful sign of the times this was? The first need, before any progress can take place, is the realisation of wrongdoing and of the necessity for a change to different methods. Once this realisation is strong enough people will set themselves to discover a better way, and of course they will succeed.

There always must be a better way of controlling world behaviour than through violence, either collective or individual. In fact the way lies ready to hand, and is simple in character. It has already been imperfectly attempted under the name of 'sanctions'. It would consist of putting any nation who transgressed against peace and freedom into 'Coventry'. Such action, which could only be taken under complete international co-operation, such as eventually the United Nations will command, could be planned to suit every situation. It is easy to see that once any nation was convinced that such action was immediately available and inevitable, should she disobey international law, she would never dare to do so.

Gandhi and others have proved how much can be accomplished by intelligent passive resistance or action, without violence or bloodshed. Such action would be still more effective if undertaken under governmental authority. Large-scale intelligent co-operation would be the major need, coupled with the realisation of that which is already possible. What is it that prevents this realisation? We suggest that because people today most-ly live a life dependent on the slaughter and exploitation of the animal kingdom, on the resultant indulgence in alcohol, tobacco and drugs which this brings, together with complete loss of the natural instincts for the correct way of feeding, they have clogged up and inhibited even their most elementary intelligence. They cannot face up to thinking things out for themselves, taking decisions, and giving up any of their many indulgences. The inadequacy of the world public authorities in face of the gallant and dire need of Hungary showed up the befogged unpreparedness by which humanity is still gripped. And on the other hand the world-wide protest which was everywhere aroused told of the inherent goodwill which was struggling for expression.

One sees today a world public at the cross-roads, at the point of the change-over from involutionary to evolutionary impulse. The terrible emotional pressure which is speeding up the tempo at the core of their beings is expressing itself in some cases in forms of hysteria, such as pop-star worship. Yet it is this same pressure which is to bring about atomic fission within the human being, so that a higher rate of vibration can take over, bringing new awareness and new orientation to those who, through pity and compassion and a yearning for the good and the real, have burned away much of the dross within, and cleared the channels for the living fire of cosmic evolution to take possession of them.

Thus many of us will become gradually aware that we have undergone a change from the inside outwards. This change will at first be too subtle for us to be fully awake to its significance. It will show itself in a variety of ways, and in all the aspects of our lives. Our *self-importance* will appear to have suffered an eclipse, as also the importance of so many habits and possessions hitherto considered indispensable. We may even feel dispossessed, disoriented, unable to apply ourselves any longer to our safe job and our many habitual hobbies and distractions. We may feel a deep loneliness within, in spite of family and friends. We may feel a terrible dissatisfaction with others, the world or ourselves. All these symptoms could be the signs of the increasing pull and power of the soul within us, which is reflecting more and more strongly the light of evolution, and the rays from those cosmic Beings which stimulate our inner core towards that crisis, that bursting asunder of our invisible bonds, that amazing emancipation into the life of atomic energy, of spiritual and material fulfilment.

Of course in many cases our personalities may with terror and stubbornness resist this great adventure. But evolution is inevitable. Such resistance and self-repression will result in nervous disease and in abnormality. Sometimes a person can, through the use of his mental powers only, achieve the conquest and control of invisible energies, whilst remaining unattached to the soul's influence. Such a dangerous situation produces an 'evil genius', an abnormally unbalanced character such as Hitler became. In the old days such power was described as Black Magic.

The Black Magician was one who wielded atomic power in ways belonging to the involutionary impulse, for personal aid and aggrandisement, for the persecution of others and for the satisfaction of greed or lust, or for destructive activities. Whereas the White Magician was one who sought spiritually oriented atomic power in the interests of others, and whose efforts were always bent towards healing and constructive evolutionary progress.

Each one of us, in however small a degree, is either a Black or a White Magician, because our every thought and radiation takes its place in the balance for either good or evil in the world. If all the thoughts, feelings and words that we have radiated throughout our lives came back to roost and we were faced with them, how much of a helpful nature would we see, either for brother man, animal, plant or planet? Yet surely, at the end of our life the sum total of our radiatory influences will be required of us? When our essence, our 'ego', is finally set free from our coat of flesh, we will exist in the medium, sphere or atomic strata of the thought and emotional worlds. We may still be connected by vibrational rate with all our radiated thoughts and emotions. We *may* still be a prisoner to that which we have built which is more lasting than the flesh.

Throughout this century the vast volume of work done by the Spiritualists would appear to prove this point. Apparently the preoccupations of the 'dear departed' do not necessarily broaden with his escape from fleshly toils! He may still be a prisoner of all his past thought habits. On the other hand, if he is a seeker, he may contact a wealth of information and experience, whose validity will of course depend upon the powers of his own orientation. Everything in life has its imitators and imitations. An art connoisseur of poor calibre will be deceived by imitations of the great masters. A seeker in the realms of the ethers will be deceived by imitations of those divine states of being which he may long to contact. Such imitations could even be built up by the still subconscious part of his own mind, if he had not succeeded in integrating himself into a 'whole' person whilst still in the flesh.

The many contradictory and voluminous descriptions and prognostications and teachings given out by disembodied people through their collaboration with 'mediums' would, if we accepted the validity of such phenomena, give us much food for thought. They would show us how important it may be for us to prepare, whilst still in the flesh, for our own future from the moment of our so-called death, which would appear to be really a birth into a still more intensive and closely packed realm of being. If it is possible we would surely like to free ourselves from the tight mental imprisonment which we have created, rather than take it with us into the next phase of living. But how could this possibly be done? Would it be too complicated a process and beyond our powers?

The accumulation of wrong (involutionary) thinking and feeling which we have put forth all our lives is attached to us by the law of similar vibrations. As long as we continue to repeat a thought or rely on it, we feed its magnetic power, we build it up into a strong 'thought-form'. The agglomeration of all our created thought-forms is of course imbued with a certain life of its own, and is attached to us permanently until we find ways of effecting a change.

This great composite thought-form, which grows up with each human being, was called by the ancient esotericists or psychologists the 'Dweller on the Threshold', because it barred the way to transmutation into a higher state of awareness. This Dweller has to be faced and tackled before any spiritual emancipation is possible. It has to be dissolved.

How is this done?

Obviously in the first place by not feeding any more those thoughts of ambition, envy, greed, self-pity, criticism, resentment, rage and so on, of which it is

composed. Such thoughts must be faced and discontin-
ued. Repression, however, will only crystallise them.
They must, instead, be replaced or reoriented to their
evolutionary aspects, in which self-pity becomes
compassion for all life, envy becomes worship, ambition
becomes devotion, greed becomes endeavour, criticism
becomes understanding, resentment becomes accep-
tance, and rage becomes love. It is only by developing
the 'good' complementary of each 'evil' thought-form
that its vibration can be gradually modified, heightened
and eventually transmuted. Thus, without any repression or condemnation, we can, through the practice of
'white magic' (or thought-control for constructive
evolutionary purpose), deliberately face and change
our ways of thinking and feeling in order not to destroy
but to transmute the 'Dweller on the Threshold', so
that it, and its vibrationary tentacles stretching through
space, can become a force for good, and lose its crystallised, imprisoning and involutionary form. This force
for good has been given a name: 'The Angel of the
Presence'.

Thus we will find, when this work is accomplished,
that not only have we set ourselves free from a prison
which might have housed us long after 'death', but we
have paid off the debt of our life-long wrong influences,
and created instead our own quota of good in this
mysterious world. This is working with the true unseen
atomic energy in its subtlest and most powerful form.
If we all did this, it would obviously transform the world
both visible and invisible. Herein lies the secret which
would be the only answer to the mighty *world* 'Dweller
on the Threshold' which is clouding men's minds today
and obstructing them from creating a perfectly possible
Paradise on their long-suffering host, the planet.

From the dimmest reaches of history human beings

have been aware of the science of self-purification and transmutation. The ancient mystics founded systems in many lands by means of which this could be achieved. We know of course that these systems were usually built round the practices of meditation and ascetic living, including fasting, dieting, breathing exercises and posture, and the study of spiritual teachings. Meditation itself was divided into several phases—concentration, meditation, contemplation and adoration.* It was an intensive process carefully designed to melt away the heavier crystallisations of the atoms of body, emotions and mind; and also to dissolve the accumulated thought fixations which formed the individual 'Dweller'. An earnest student who finally realised the values of real living, and came to put the spiritual angle first and all-important in his life, became a disciple of Yoga, or its equivalent in the race or culture to which he belonged. His whole attention was then focused on the attainment of a state of purity and spiritual awareness; in other words, a condition in which all the grosser atoms within him had disintegrated and reassembled on a higher rate of vibration, thus opening up to him a world of new experiences and powers altogether.

In the study of Yoga there were five main paths in the one general system, arranged to suit the needs of different types of students. There was the Râja or King Yoga, which endeavoured to achieve union with the Divine Will. There was Gnana Yoga, in which union was achieved through knowledge leading to wisdom. There was Karma Yoga or the study of right action. There was Bhakta Yoga, achieving union through love. Finally, there was Hatha Yoga, the study of physical control and courage. Hatha Yoga was the basis for all the other Yogas, and Râja Yoga was the final flowering. Bhakta

* See *The Fifth Dimension*

K

Yoga was for the mystic and emotional type, Karma Yoga was for the active and practical type, and Gnana Yoga was for the intellectual.

The early Christian groups taught self-purification. Christ said, 'Only through prayer and fasting shalt thou come unto Me!' He enjoined His disciples to keep themselves unspotted from the world and to live with great frugality. The Buddha practised and taught a life of complete dedication to spiritual growth and self-purification, as well as harmlessness to all creatures.

All these things we have heard. But because we are only half alive we have not been able to grasp their implications. It has been rather like trying to teach a blind man about colours. Our heavy vibrations cut us off from a teeming vibrant world of exciting and wonderful happenings, and to us it simply does not yet exist. We are shut in, clogged up, bogged down, weighed under as the result of an utterly false, damaging and destructive way of living, feeling and thinking. At times we may have vague glimmerings of the marvellous life outside our chrysalis, tiny experiences of fractions of the real love, light, radiance, power, awareness and ecstasy in that pulsating world from which we have insulated ourselves. But such words as glory, enlightenment, love, wisdom and worship remain only *words* with us, rendered parrot-like from repetition and having no resemblance to the glorious realities which lie behind them.

Indeed, as Krishnamurti has said, we are not yet even real human beings, but frightened, self-inhibited chrysalides afraid to emerge.

How *can* we break out? What kind of action will set us free?

The required action is utterly simple but extraordinarily difficult for all of us, else obviously we had already accomplished it. It consists in balancing the mind so that it is completely *impartial*, and then regarding quite calmly and fearlessly our every mental and emotional reaction. If we are quite quiet whilst doing this our 'still small voice' will show us instantly *ourselves as we are*. There is a curious law of nature which decrees that when once the fire of the unbiased mind has been focused on to a thought-form, a habit of mind, a crystallised vibration which is involutionary or undesirable, it will disintegrate, burn up, and return to the circle of force which projected it. It is exactly the same process as that which occurs when the imprisoned core of an atom is impinged upon by a stimulating influence. It warms up, expands, finally becomes explosive, and is either shattered or shoots out that whose departure will allow it to transmute into a freer, lighter and less crystallised state.

If we impinge the radiance of our soul and will upon our undesirable thought-crystallisations, we shall produce a process of combustion within them. This may mean horrible mental conflict, resistance and indecision whilst this disintegration is taking place. But if our will-to-good and will-to-freedom is strong and enduring, the process will carry through to its inevitable result. Suddenly one day we will become aware that we are free from that particular bondage, we will find that the fear or the envy or the fixed obsession is simply no longer there. We cannot even imitate or revive it with any success. We are free of it. We are intrinsically different.

Meditation rightly conducted consists in carefully setting the mind free of all its bad habits, its preconceived ideas and fixations, its materialistic preoccupations. The practices of Yoga, realising that the body is an expression of the state of the mind, endeavour at the same time to release the corresponding muscular and nervous fixations in the body, and to cleanse the blood-stream of all the impurities due to wrong or involu-tionary living. Diet is naturally of the utmost importance because *atomic nourishment must be taken into the body of a degree of fineness corresponding to the state of transmutation that the person is achieving*. We would not use the same heavy oil with which we oil a great engine to clean a delicate wrist-watch. If we can perceive the obvious in this respect, then why not the equally obvious in regard to our own mechanism?

An aspirant or spiritual student who has intelligently transmuted his bodily atoms, his emotional and his mental atoms *concurrently with each other* can hope for remarkable results. From having nourished himself on the coarser and more poisonous atoms found for example in flesh foods and crude starches, he trains his body to take its nourishment from ever finer and subtler foods. He soon comes face to face with the fact that the human body was built to be nourished mainly by fruits and the grains and the green leaf. If his reorientation to-wards a new and better or more natural way of living takes place in all aspects of his being, evenly and completely, he will eventually find himself fully nour-ished on a small fraction of the amount which he 'needed' before, and that fraction would most likely be mainly fruit. The nourishment from fruit is a living electrical essence, needing little or no digestion, and leaving little or no residue or 'ash' within the body. The essences, aromas and alcohols from fruit constitute the nearest thing to that nourishment which the cells can draw from the cosmic rays. Feeding upon fruit en-courages the cells of the body to learn to nourish themselves completely and directly upon the subtle essences of the cosmic rays, which contain, as we have seen, all required substances in their finest form.

By the time a person has so reoriented his own being that he uses up no stores of energy on undesirable thinking, wrong movement, or crude nourishment, he has arrived at a state where he *could* subsist entirely from the cosmic rays, the Breath of God. This has actually happened many times throughout history, and there are even cases of it today. Many of the saints were able to live with little or no food, and sometimes, as in the case of Theresa Neumann, with neither food nor drink.* There have been many instances of transmuted people who through the practice of the 'white magic' of selfless spiritual adoration have demonstrated miracles within themselves and have also been able to heal others.

Not only are such results possible to any one of us, but they would appear to be the natural development which lies far ahead of humanity when it finally becomes 'adult' and takes responsibility for its own fulfilment. Nor is mystical rapture necessary in order to lift men above normal bodily needs. In India there was the case of an ordinary domesticated young woman who for many years has lived in health and strength without eating and drinking, and who seemed very bonny from the photographs of her which have appeared more than once in the press. The Indian doctors could find nothing abnormal about her.

We have had examples of this kind of phenomenon generation after generation. But their implications have failed to register with us. Like the horse who is taken to the water, we refuse to drink—in this case, of the waters of life! Until the moment arrives when our souls have reflected so much inner light into the core of our personalities that the uncomfortable process of expansion and combustion begins to take place within us, our

* See publications by the Natural Science Society, Orlando, Florida.

moment has not arrived. But when it does arrive, if we are aware of what is happening through such a study as we have here undertaken, we will be able to co-operate with hope and joy in the radioactive process which is so painfully coming into action. Thus, instead of ending up in an asylum or a nerve clinic, as we might otherwise have done, we can with confidence face the prospect of a glorious unfoldment.

12

A glance through history

THE existence of atomic energy has always been known to certain of the intelligentsia of all races. Aspirants to a pure life hoped thereby to train and transmute their bodies to the point where they deliberately could absorb and feed upon the cosmic rays, whose substance was known in India, for instance, as Prana.

In most ancient civilisations there was a firmly established system for living the life of regeneration. This usually included a fleshless or humane diet, because of course the act of eating flesh and of killing or of causing others to kill for you was considered to hold down the personal vibrations to a low and coarse level wherein *true* spiritual development would be impossible. And when we consider the pass to which a flesh-eating world has come at the present time, we may find it rather significant. We may be reminded once more of God's Covenant with Noah, and His words: 'But flesh with the life thereof, which is the blood thereof, shall ye not eat. And surely your blood of your lives will I require; at the hand of every beast will I require it, and at the hand of man; at the hand of every man's brother will I require the life of man' (Genesis ix, 4, 5). And in fact man pays with his blood all the time when he becomes diseased.

In India is found one of the oldest of all the systems of spiritual-ethical-physical training, known, as we have said, as Yoga. This system includes meditation, breathing, posture, diet, development of the glands and centres, and a frugal way of life. The Buddha took intensive training in Yoga before he achieved illumination. Its counterpart existed of course in all great civilisations. The Egyptian priestly tradition went back into the dimmest past. Their Book of the Dead shows an extensive postulate of the invisible development of man, of his etheric and emotional aspects, and of his glandular-planetary centres; and of the salvation offered to him by the cyclic arrival of a world messiah whom they called the 'Ever-Coming One'. In China, in Japan and in Tibet the spiritual tradition and training was equally profound and, was the essential background of daily life. We have already outlined the history of spiritual growth and spiritual teachers throughout the world, in a former book.* Such teaching has therefore always been available to those seekers who were able to look for it.

After the fall of Rome and the successive Barbarian invasions, many priceless archives of esoteric literature were destroyed, and much else was hidden away for safety. There ensued the 'Dark Ages', wherein superstition often took the place of real knowledge. Without the carefully supervised training necessary, an aspirant to the higher knowledge often made an unbalanced progress. That is to say, he developed a knowledge of how to use the mind for the control of invisible forces, *without* developing his spiritual integrity and channel for soul illumination at the same time. Therefore he worked without obeying certain fundamental esoteric laws. These insist upon harmlessness to all life, and the allowing of full liberty for development to every living creature; also the practice of service instead of exploita-

* See *The Initiation of the World.* (Rider & Co.)

tion in any form. A person who was still intent upon self-aggrandisement (involutionary living) became very dangerous when trained in esoteric knowledge. He became what was known as a 'black magician', in distinction to the 'white magician' or the one who worked always for the good of others. He was on the 'left-hand path' as opposed to the 'Right-Hand Path' or the way of illumination.

This meant that the 'black magician' sought to capture and use atomic energy and other types of force for the gain of personal power. In this way he sought not to help the mineral and animal worlds with their process of transmutation, but to capture and use their escaping energies for unworthy purposes. In the Middle or Dark Ages both men and women engaged in these pursuits. We can call to mind, for instance, the mysterious and monstrous 'left-hand' practices of some of the Medici family. Their aims were very different from those of the white magicians or Magi, for instance, who eagerly sought for the newly born Christ.

After the barbarian invasions, such practices were attempted by the less privileged classes. We know that in the case of women they became known as witches and were held in awe by the populace. Finally, they aroused such fear and hatred that they were burned to death in their thousands, as we already mentioned.

It could be said that those scientists of today who are producing atomic energy by violent means for violent ends are also on the 'left-hand path'. A few generations ago they would quite definitely have belonged in the ranks of the Black Magicians. Such a one was doomed to lengthy expurgation, it was believed, and was inadmissible to the Kingdom of Heaven. In other words he had tuned himself in to a vibrationary world of extreme unpleasantness. His vibrational allegiances and his 'Dweller on the Threshold' were such as to make enlightenment impossible for him. He remained insulated in his own darkness and in the horror of accumulated evil thought-forms.

In the ranks of both medicine and science there existed, of course, both 'black' and 'white' exponents. As always, good and evil were sometimes inextricably mixed. The foundations of all the arts and sciences were originally laid down by the ancient priestcrafts. Their work was founded upon astrology, a system which it can now be realised was nothing less than a profound study of the cosmic rays!

In early times there was no division between medicine, spiritual lore and astrology. It was all one science, the science of the knowledge of life and of the plan of the Creator. Later on the growing materialism caused science, medicine and esoteric lore to go their separate ways. The Orthodox Church also deserted all three. There ensued a period when knowledge was shut off into unconnected compartments, and this has persisted until quite recently. During this long age of separatism the separateness or individuality of man was steadily built up. All possible separateness was emphasised, including the separateness of the sexes, the separateness of the ethical and spiritual life from the business and practical life, the separateness of the emotional life from the intellectual life, and of the national life from world needs.

As we have seen, such attitudes have produced a humanity with an incoherent outlook, dislocated personalities unconnected with their own inner source, and a sceptical or indifferent approach to many fundamental aspects of living which were hitherto accepted as a matter of course. Nevertheless astrology, whose remnants are now relegated to the popular press, was the foundation upon which astronomy, medicine, law, architecture, science, music and psychology were founded; in which connection the name of Pythagoras, amongst many other geniuses, springs to mind. Many learned men of his time would seek out the early Egyptian priestcraft for the source of their information. After the era of Christ the Christian aspirants often travelled to the Egyptian desert to learn from the holy Desert Fathers (the early monks) the way of the life of purification. Pagan and Christian belief and knowledge were deliberately welded together in order to make it easier to draw the many mixed races who swarmed over Europe into the Christian fold.

The early Christians were deeply devout. They usually wished to give up privileges and possessions and seek the simple austere life of the recluse, monk or nun. The pure regenerate life was their goal to almost the same degree as it was with the eastern mystics. That is why we hear of so many miracles, healings and sainthoods achieved amongst their ranks—the ranks of the 'Right-Hand Path'. Of course the secular priesthood who attended to business, legal and social matters in the big cities were admittedly generally in a different category.

The tradition of the rightful combination of medicine with spiritual law, science and astrology was kept alive by certain learned men known as the Alchemists. They believed that behind and within all physical manifestation there was a primeval elixir, a marvellous essence that through the medium of the aether or ether imbued all living things with power, vitality and energy. They believed that this elixir had been buried most completely in the metals, and that metals were conscious living entities, who breathed, excreted, and developed. Alchemy was the 'chemistry of the all', a science taking

156 THE SECRET OF THE ATOMIC AGE

into account all aspects of life. The Alchemist sought, with the help of a traditional system preserved in the ancient archives of many civilisations, to subject a metal to processes which should gently disintegrate it into its component parts of 'body, soul and spirit' or essence, juice and salts, or solid, liquid and gas, *without losing any volatile and potent emanations.* The idea was to purify and sublimate all parts of the metal by a long and gentle process, and then bring them together again in their ultimate transmuted form. In this form they were supposed to be reduced to the very essence of metallic life, and therefore could act upon the essence of all other life, because the nearer one gets to the essence of all living things the more the barriers and differences melt away, and the more can they act upon each other.

When the Alchemists obtained their elixirs from the metals they were apparently very healing and rejuvenating medicines. They were also supposed to be able to speed up the evolution of certain metals and turn them into pure gold, which is the king of all metals, or their ultimate goal. If the reader wishes to satisfy himself as to the validity of this age-old science he must attempt to do so through his own researches into the vast literature which exists upon this subject. Certain it is that modern scientists have at this time produced gold, and transmuted and changed many elements one into another.

However, as we have said, the Alchemist sought, through a patient and most gentle process, to reduce all the parts of a metal, and therefore its atoms, to a highly purified and transmuted state, *without losing the indwelling life,* cosmic essence, 'prana' or spirit—so that the final result was to have speeded up the natural evolution of the metal by millions of years, and to capture the resultant quintessence of life *still* in physical form. This was not only atomic energy but atomic spirit also. It could act as a most powerful catalyst in speeding up the evolutionary process in other living forms. It meant working with the inner forces of life without changing their natural evolution. Whereas the nuclear physicist of today does just the opposite. By crudely violent action he bursts asunder the atoms, allowing the real life to escape, and retains for his use the raw outraged energies and explosive or poisonous products thus unnaturally produced.

Nature produces her results by the use of a long series of radiations which we know as sound, light, colour, motion, heat. Those are the architects of form, the storers and releasers of energy. These radiations could be used to produce *living* atomic energy, non-poisonous, rejuvenating and buoyant. They have always been used by those priesthoods who retained their early practical and scientifically based traditions, and who, by means of chanting, music, incense, colour and posture, succeeded in producing the release of vital energies and therefore of exaltation and sublimation within their congregations.

When the Alchemists had transmuted their metal to its ultimate stages, a succession of fragrant oils was produced whose colours ranged from crystal white to a deep ruby. The delicious and subtle flower-fragrances given out by these oils, composed as they were of nothing but metal, was the sign that the soul and spirit of the metal had been finally released. That part of an entity which is quite purified and of the highest vibration is always fragrant. Fragrance is that subtle volatile emanation which is so near to the spiritual world that it is often the expression of it, and indicates its presence. There have been many cases when the body of a saint, years after his death, gave out such a fragrant and healing perfume that pilgrims came from afar to be blessed and rejuvenated by it. It is claimed that the presence of certain noble beings of the invisible world can be detected by their delicious perfume.

When a person has lived what is known as a pure life for a number of years, abstaining from all unconstructive thoughts and activities, and eating the living natural fruits of the earth, his body becomes completely fragrant in *all* its functions. A little reflection will show how far the average man is from such a normal state for which biologically he was built. Can we imagine what it must feel like to have a perfectly pure and healthy body, which is able deliberately to sustain itself upon all those things which are nearest to the spiritual essence of life, those substances which are the expression of atomic energy in its most released and subtle form—substances such as the cosmic rays themselves which are the highest expression of the mineral world, and the subtle emanations from flowers and fruits which are the highest expression of the plant world?

Man was built biologically as a fruit-eater. Even in his degenerated state of today he can still be rescued very often from an 'incurable' condition of disease by a fruit diet. Naturally much depends on the metabolism which he produces in his body by his thoughts and actions. If these deplete his energies and lower his rate of vibration he will tend to seek the rapid unnatural stimulants given by the poisons in gross food, and the vicious circle will start all over again.

But the man (or woman) who 'overcomes', and who establishes himself in a free (from self-centredness) and pure (non-exploiting) way of living, will in the end become a fragrant fountain of atomic energy—not the crude undeveloped outraged atomic energy of the laboratory, but the true natural fulfilment of that mystery, the human being. In this state he will be impervious to heat or cold, because he carries his own thermostatic control about with him. This is a condition which such people as the Tibetan Llamas have often demonstrated. He will also be impervious to poisons because his body contains such potent solvents with which to deal with them. Yogis are known to be able to resist the most deadly of poisons. He will also be able to exist if required without food, drink or even oxygen. This is because he has developed himself and his cells to the point when he *can subsist directly upon the cosmic rays*. Yogis who are buried alive for days are able to do this, although even if imperfectly, because of course the cosmic rays can penetrate through any substances in which they have been entombed.

As we have said, the geniuses of modern science are proving to the public today, although not deliberately, that so-called miracles were neither superstitious hoaxes nor unexplainable abnormalities, but simply the outcome of a competent and developed approach to the powerful inner laws of nature.

The ideal of a purified life, free from the taint of blood or the guilt of exploitation, was recognised and embraced by many of our well-known geniuses, although, as we have said, the fact was usually not emphasised, as it was mostly uninteresting to either a materialistic press or a self-indulgent public. Now things are changing. People would be astonished and inspired to know how many of the great figures whom they so much admire in the history of art, literature and science were also ardent supporters of the purified life.

For instance, Richard Wagner was the author of several large volumes of essays,* in which he made a powerful plea that man should cease to be a beast of prey, and should turn to a life of compassion and

* See 'The Millenium Guild' literature, U.S.A.

responsibility towards all living creatures. He wrote: 'When first it dawned on human wisdom that the same thing breathed in animals as in mankind, it appeared too late to avert the curse which, ranging ourselves with the beasts of prey, we seemed to have called down upon us through the taste of animal food; disease and misery of every kind, to which we did not see mere vegetable-eating man exposed. The insight thus obtained led further to the consciousness of a deep-seated guilt in our earthly being; it moved those fully seized therewith to turn aside from all that stirs the passions, through total abstinence from animal food. To these wise men the mystery of the world unveiled itself as a restless tearing into pieces, to be restored to restful unity by nothing save compassion.' The wise men to whom Wagner referred in his writings were Plutarch, Hesiod, Senaca, Pythagoras, who are only a few of the leaders of men who preached and practised the humane and purified life, including the vegetarian diet. Wagner wrote earnestly and poignantly enough to strike a chord of regeneration in the hardest heart, but so far his writings are practically unknown, especially to the most ardent admirers of his music. The same can be said of Tolstoy. Vegetarianism was one of the fundamental principles of Tolstoy's life. In his published records he has referred to it as the 'acid test of humanitarianism' and the 'first step in the road to clean living'. As for Leonardo da Vinci, he also tried hard to guide people to a nobler way of living, and declared: 'From an early age I have abjured the use of meat, and the time will come when men will look upon the murder of animals as they now look upon the murder of men.' Among others who claimed to be vegetarians in principle and practice were Ovid, Plato, Buddha, Milton, Rousseau, Voltaire, Darwin, Shelley, Schopenhauer, Nietzsche, Swedenborg, Maeterlinck,

General Booth, Paganini, Maxim Gorky, Blake, Marie
Corelli, Gandhi, and George Bernard Shaw. These are
only a few names from very much longer lists which
have been compiled.

Today there are so many thousands of books and
pamphlets pleading for the abolishment of the inhuman
slavery of animals by mankind that there is no need to
say more about it in this chapter. Anyone who is in the
least interested will find themselves snowed under with
copious appeals to help in the liberation of the animal
world. Indeed, as Tolstoy said, it is the necessary first
step before any real regeneration can take place in man.
The Early Church Fathers have indicated in their
writings that some of the disciples and early Christians
were vegetarians, and the belief was held that the
sacrifice of Christ was made to expiate the collective
human guilt of murder in respect of all God's creatures.
Many feel that the Christian faith would obtain a new
lease of life if some such realisation were courageously
approached today.

How can there be any regeneration or development
so long as human beings deliberately shut their eyes to
the fact that so many of the substances which they use
are only obtained at the cost of inhuman cruelty, and
exploitation of living creatures, of their fellow-men, of
the tree and plant kingdom and of the soil? In order to
shut all these realisations out of one's mind it is necessary, is it not, to render oneself half conscious, and to
dislocate completely one's integrity and one's clear-
sightedness. This results in the innumerable neuroses to
which man is a prey today. This is so because human
beings are *by nature* honest, generous, keen to know and
to grow, and above all to take responsibility. It is their
'Dweller on the Threshold', their past, *the mind*, which
is supporting itself on a cushion of habit and self-

L

protection, which is blocking their way. That is expressed in the age-old axiom: 'The mind is the enemy of the real.'

Truth is ever-changing living movement. It is not static. Therefore only a mind which is regularly *emptied* and held open is capable of taking in the constantly modifying truth which men have ever vainly sought, because they wanted something which they could add to all their static mental possessions, their little stock of mental gramophone-records.

Not only is it the truth which will set men free, but it is only a freed mind which can perceive the truth. This is the virtuous (not vicious!) circle into which we have to reorient ourselves in order to become a channel for life's flowing atomic energy.

13

What is atomic energy?

WE can now ask ourselves whether we have reached the answer to our search as to what atomic energy really is, or if there is a still more fascinating secret to be discovered about it?

We know, of course, that atomic energy is the ultimate essence—or the nearest thing to the ultimate essence—of all life. But that does not explain exactly what it *is*. If it is so near to or a part of the innermost essence, then it must be the nearest equivalent of that which we call 'God': Divinity Itself. That seems obvious enough, but it still does not exactly tell us what in substance and effect atomic energy *is*—or does it?

What have we been told about the actual character of God? Anything definite? Yes, we have been told that God is Love. But that has seemed to us unthinking people a grand, vague word, which we sometimes connect with the puny little possessive attraction which we feel for those on whom our social happiness depends. This is putting it unkindly, and does not of course apply to everyone. But it must be emphasised that the conception of the character of love which is held by a self-centred person differs radically from that which would be held by a selfless person.

I say *would be* because selflessness is so rare that we find it intensely difficult even to imagine the mental attitude of a truly selfless person. Let us, however, try.

A selfless person is one who has broken down the thick shell of preoccupation with and fear for personal security; of selfconsciousness and therefore sensitivity to 'ill-treatment', 'ill-luck' and all outer attitudes to itself; of envy, greed, resentment, ambition, lust, impatience and a score of other reflexes of selfishness; all of which are permeated with the subconscious sense of guilt which they all bring. Think what a hard, complex, impenetrable shell of thought-fixations such a condition encloses us in. If we should manage by some miracle of the will to break out of it we would at first feel quite naked, helpless, strange and dislocated from all our former preoccupations.

But later, as we became accustomed to our new condition we would begin to observe, little by little, the complete change which had taken place in our relationship with everything about us. Hitherto we had considered every entity which we contacted solely as regards its relationship, beneficial or otherwise, to our own personality. But, now that we have relinquished and melted away that personality, or rather our consciousness of it, there is *no adjustment to be made* with anything which we contact. There is no longer 'ourselves versus the object of contact'. There is merely the object. Therefore we, for the first time, see it exactly *as it is*, unprejudiced by any of our own thought-forms. In other words, we are immediately identified with it. Our radiations link up at once and freely with all similar vibrations in the object of contact. Not only do we see it as it is; we feel how it feels; suffer as it suffers; and understand as it understands; and this is the true meaning of *love*.

The radiations emanating from ourselves which perform this linking and identifying action are those of our atomic energy. In other words, it is the act of untrammelled transmutation of the finer atoms of our body, mind and emotions, propelled by the atomic energy of their own release, which produces that subtle high-powered radiation which is at one with all its counter-parts throughout nature.

The 'Love' that is God, is just that, the underlying radiation which identifies with all and therefore unites all, harmonises all, and conduces to the rightful co-operation and symbiosis between all living things. Therefore, when we have achieved within ourselves, through a purified life, the true release and fulfilment of atomic energy, we have achieved *love,* that actual quality and activity so little understood so far by man. We have achieved love to the extent that we have *become* love in action and in embodiment.

The ancient sages told us not only that God is Love, but that this particular solar system is founded upon the 'cosmic ray of love' and therefore can only be fulfilled and understood by means of that mysterious radiation, which is the root and fountain of all its being. Therefore the ultimate expression of atomic energy is love. Its character, and the way of its fulfilment and its unlimited power, is, in the last analysis, the demonstration of that fountain-head of our existence, which one day we will understand, and which meanwhile is almost completely veiled from us by the thought-fixation which we attach to the word LOVE.

Surely this conclusion of our search is a curious one with which to face the scientists who are busy on the brilliant but so far unscientific (because unloving in the true sense) methods of releasing atomic energy? If the way of evolution on this planet is the way of love or, understanding unification, in which violence and coer-civeness can have no part, then, in order not to bring about those unfortunate reactions which are due to the outraging of natural laws, a way must be found of releasing atomic energy which is in line with evolution. Only through such means can we hope to build a clean, healthy and vital world, and cease from adding to the filth, poison and degeneracy resulting from present methods.

What then are the forces which could be used harmlessly and constructively by scientists, in order to release atomic energy?

If I appear to be criticising modern scientific methods I would make it clear that I am *not* criticising the scientists. Surely their brilliance, devotion and ingenuity beggars all praise. The nature of the methods which they use is due to the fact that neither from their parents, their schools, their church nor the State have they been given that background from which they could have achieved a different approach to their work. Nor can one specifically blame either church or school for the quite inadequate ethical and psychological bases of their training. Church, State and school are upheld by men and women drawn from our own ranks, and approved collectively and individually by us all. The blame and the responsibility for all their activities comes home to roost with each and every one of *us*. However unimportant we may feel, and however much we may try to shirk this challenge, we cannot deny, even according to the picture presented in these chapters, that the influence of our habitual thinking produces the ingredients of the situation in the world today.

Our thoughts circle the earth day after day. They strengthen and amalgamate with all similar thoughts in the ether. The sum total of all thinking is that which will orient all receptive intelligences, man or animal, according to their capacity. Millions were trained by their parents to be obedient and unquestioning. There were few who thought of resisting the crystallised thought-forms so heavily impinging upon them. Those who now *do* so will have the arduous but thrilling task of finding an alternative, and of discovering the realities hidden behind the façade of modern human living.

Is it possible to conceive of any more desirable methods which scientists could use for the release of atomic energy, methods which could be used harmlessly, without producing poisonous by-products, and which would be in line with natural evolution? What, for instance, are the forces which nature causes to impinge upon living matter and bring about stimulation, growth, and finally transmutation? They are mostly in the form of radiations. These radiations occur as a long ladder of sequences,* which are recognisable by us as sound, whose vibrations range up to roughly 33,000 per second; electricity, whose vibrations are in the neighbourhood of 1,000 million per second; heat, which vibrates in the neighbourhood of 200 billion per second; light and colour, at 500 billion; and X-ray at two trillion vibrations per second. Above these we find the subtle complex radiations of perfume, and finest of all the series of vibrations given out by mental and emotional activities.

This long range of vibrations divides up into octaves of seven, each octave having its overtones, and also its correspondences in every other octave in the range. At the bottom of the scale are the octaves of crystallised atoms, the minerals. At the top of the scale are the octaves of *qualities*, and these are given expression by the mental and emotional activities as well as by the character of every living entity in all kingdoms.

It is possible to select a mineral from the lowest octaves and pick out its correspondence, its vibrational

* See *The Finding of the Third Eye.*

affinity, from the range of sound notes, from the range of colours, of perfumes, of electrical rays, of qualities or characteristics, and of cosmic rays. That is to say that any given chemical element will be found to be the crystallisation of a radiation which at its successively higher rates of vibration will be recognisable as a sounded note, a definite colour, a certain perfume, an electrical emanation or force, a quality or characteristic expressible by emotional or mental activity, and finally a certain cosmic ray.

It is the successive gentle crystallisation from a cosmic ray to an electrical radiation, and from these to a colour, and from thence to a sound, which produces the ultimate molecule of solid matter. The return journey from the molecule to the cosmic ray must be accomplished by the same means. It was the 'WORD', or sound, which created the physical world. Therefore sound must be used for the gentle and natural disintegration of physical matter and the release of atomic energy. It would be necessary to discover the given note which is the affinity or unlocking agent for a given element or substance. We know that a glass vessel can be shattered by sounding into it its own note. Each one of us has his own keynote, which if applied to us correctly would have a radically constructive or destructive effect upon us according to the timbre used.

After the scientist has allocated the correct note or sound to be applied to the substance from which he wishes to release atomic energy, he would next have to discover the correct colour. The application of this would affect a different stratum in the bodies of the atoms concerned. Further to this would be the application of electrical radiations whose affinity with the atoms under treatment had been determined.

This would mean that all grades and parts of the

atom, such as the proton, the neutron, the electron and the strata of atmosphere, would each receive that type of stimulation to which it would respond. A natural expansion and separation would then occur. The atom would *enjoy* what was happening to it, and would co-operate in its own painless liberation with the eagerness of natural growth, so that *no* angry poisonous by-products were formed.

The production of atomic energy by such means would be slower, gentler, less expensive by far, and could take place on a more widespread scale. The quantity produced would be far greater, without being concentrated largely in one place. The whole process would be devoid of the unpleasant dangers which accompany present methods.

It is likely that the use of colour, sound (and therefore form patterns) and other radiations on the vibratory scale for the release of atomic energy will eventually bring in a still newer era of nuclear physics, which will be harmless and evolutionary in its effects. By that time we will have learned to apply the same principles to ourselves. By means of colour, sound, perfume, the rhythm which we are enabled to apply by scientific breathing, and the radiations projected by our own mental apparatus, we will release our own atomic energy, and rebuild every atom and cell in our own bodies.

Various efforts are made at present which use a fraction of these possibilities, such as those applied by movements like Christian Science, or by the yogis, or by certain psychic and occult groups. In each case results are obtained. But an understanding of the complete process of transmutation to which evolution on this planet is geared, and of its wonderful implications, would give humanity such an inspiring and glorious goal for which to work, that a real renaissance of the spirit could be evoked.

This is one aspect of the future as opposed to that of the Atom Bomb. *We cannot have them both.* A humanity which deliberately can countenance the mass production of the most horrible weapon of destruction yet invented, is totally unfit to reap any of the spiritual and vital benefits which atomic energy *could* offer. It neither wants them nor understands them. Nevertheless, humanity stands at present at the cross-roads of a choice between these two ways. That choice will *have* to be made. Either the peoples will flounder into an atomic war of self-annihilation; or they will hover on the border of it in a state of fear, bankruptcy, want and disease. Or they will rouse up their courage, face facts, give up their fatal reliance on violence, and turn over a new page in history whereon their discovery of the true way of living could be written in letters of gold.

This would not be an act performed by a few of those in authority. It has first to be accomplished, from the spirit outwards, by you, by me, and by our neighbours all around the world. We must help and inspire each other. We must stand together for a new life. Not all of us can do this, of course, but only a very small percentage. But that percentage, because it will aspire to the use of the higher vibrations, can become all-powerful, although in a selfless way. It will have the backing of Divine Will, and of the planetary soul, with all the mysterious aid which that will bring. It will set up a new battery of power in the world, circulating radiations and waves around it in ever-increasing potency, until the day will come when it overbalances the involutionary radiations. On that day the world Dweller on the Threshold will finally crumble and melt away. Humanity will see across that threshold into the etheric world and the realms of reality. The great revelation will then come of the meaning of Christ's words: 'Lo, I am with you always.'

So that with which we are brought face to face at the end of our search is the discovery that the atomic energy which is being sought with so much scientific effort, and that Love of God which has been personified for us by the Christ, and which should be the goal for each of us, are very much akin. In nature that love, or atomic energy, is radiated to us by the sun. For the sun is the *heart* of this great atom, our solar system. And the heart is proverbially the seat of love. *Therefore in the heart of the solar system of each tiny atom resides the fiery mighty force of love!* It is that which the scientist is attacking and approaching when he bursts asunder the atom. That mighty force which is holding the world together, that terrific pull of attraction, that wonderful law of interdependence, is nothing less than love, the love of the Creator for His creation. It is one of the aspects of Deity. Another aspect is light or illumination, that which also illumines the mind and makes a living being conscious. The first aspect is that of power, the energy which initiates all vibration and movement.

Therefore love, light and power are the three aspects of life within the atom, loosely termed atomic energy. But the greatest of these, truly the heart of matter, is love.

14

The secret revealed

I T is perhaps with a queer kind of shock that we come upon the ultimate secret which lies in wait for us within the atom. For it is nothing less than the discovery of love—love in its essence and in its reality.

We may not at first recognise it. We may choose to call it by another name. But if we are practical enough to put two and two together, to dovetail all the aspects of this great force of attraction, we will find that it is the one and self-same force, whether it is drawing together the nucleus of an atom, the marriages of the elements into compounds, the mysterious bonds within solar systems, the attraction between living creatures, or the turning of all life towards the sun.

The same grand silent force is acting as the support and the integrator of all life; bringing fulfilment to all who respond to and align with it. It is of course stepped down, decimated and imprisoned by the littleness of human minds, which so often succeed in reversing this force to its negative side. For every quality inherent in the world has its negative side. That is to say it can be reversed to its *involutionary* aspect. When this happens, love or evolutionary attraction becomes greed, lust, exclusiveness; light or illumination becomes over-intellectualism, craftiness and cunning: integrity becomes intolerance; devotion becomes fanaticism; learning becomes obsession. All this happens so long as the 'I', or involutionary self-centredness, holds sway.

After release from the 'I', all qualities within the personality reorient to their positive and evolutionary aspect. Everything is seen from a new viewpoint, a selfless and therefore a greatly enlarged one. Love is experienced and understood in quite a different way and its stupendous secret lies revealed. We can see the great pattern of world history, wherein the descent into matter has been achieved through separatism, and the conquest and transmutation of matter is being accomplished through unification, identification, integration, co-operation—alias love!

With our finite and unpractised minds we cannot yet hope to unravel the mystery of *why* all this happened. We must walk before we may run. But we *can* undeniably perceive the pattern thus far if we give our minds a little preliminary exercise.

It was the negative working of the great love force which caused creatures to devour each other in their struggle for self-preservation and self-security. Between loving and devouring there has been a hardly perceptible division throughout involutionary history. Through greed the bacteria in the body devour the living cells when they get a chance or when the owner of that body produces conditions which allow of it. Through greed members of one family will exploit, make use of and psychically devour each other. Throughout all the kingdoms of nature the parasite and the carnivore exist side by side with the evolutionary creatures who give, provide and construct with everything that they take from life.

We all know how we can condition our outlook with 'wishful thinking'. Those who wish to avoid facing up to the challenge of evolution and transmutation can easily play over the mental gramophone records which recount that 'nature is red in tooth and claw', that 'there will always be wars', that 'human nature will never change', and that 'the animals were given to man for his use'. Such unthinking platitudes allow people to lag behind in the involutionary class, and reap the terrible harvest of stupidity, disease and cruelty which this brings.

For those, however, who are courageously striving forward towards the goal of 'second birth', towards transmutation into a new body and mind, and a new world of realities, there comes a new way of living, feeling, thinking—the way of love, that love which is almost unrecognisable from our former conception of it. For the *heart* of every flame is white and cold!

Let us look into the future for a moment and imagine where this new way of life will lead us as soon as it gains enough momentum. The impulses which it will send forth will incline all the activities of living in the direction of co-operation, sharing, fusing, unifying. The involutionary impulse inclined towards separatism, departmentalism, infinite division into self-sufficient units working and fighting for self-security at the cost of everything around. This caused nations to build themselves up at the cost of their neighbours. It caused commerce to be founded on the profit system. It caused education to be split up into dissociated compartments. It caused religion, psychology, medicine, law, science and the arts all to go their separate ways. Everything was in conflict with or exploiting everything else. This resulted in the totality of war, even world war.

Thus was expressed the love of the self, which is the reverse side of the real or universal love. Up to the present it has outweighed the growing amount of good-will, generosity and self-sacrifice which has been rapidly emerging all over the world, and which is bound eventually to catch up with it. When that happens, and when the change over is finally achieved, we will see that all these self-centred impulses have been reversed into group-centred or world-centred reactions.

It will then be realised that family 'loyalty' and national 'patriotism' are only good so long as they do not isolate one from 'world patriotism' and loyalty to all one's fellow-creatures in all kingdoms of nature. The intense absorption which we have for those people who are a part of our family circle, our career or our social clique—in other words, who contribute to our possessions or well-being—will dissolve into the larger absorption with the whole family of mankind. People will be inspired with a wish to serve the *whole* cause of progress. For humanity as a *whole* will be reaching maturity, the stage at which they feel the need to take responsibility, to work out their own salvation, and to put self-indulgence and childish acquiescence to authority behind them.

The twenty-first century will mark the majority or coming of age of the human family taken as a unit. Although there will still be the 'masses', or the body of humanity, the 'head' or the intelligentsia will have awakened out of the long period of adolescent emotionalism, and out of the more recent period of scientific intellectualism, and will be ready to progress from there to the world of synthesised *realities*, real values, real laws of living, and the real goal of evolution. It will be a spiritual renaissance, in which spirit comes at last into its own and is recognised as the fundamental mainspring of science, government, education and health, instead of as something vague and separate from it all.

The time will come when the fundamental laws of nature will be used as the foundation for daily living, instead of being obstinately defied as they are today.

The new astrology of the cosmic rays will be amalgamated with the ancient wisdom. This will bring into view the secret of the GROUP. It will be recognised that intelligence and activity have been split up on this solar system into twelve major qualities or influences. Every entity in any of the kingdoms of nature belongs for the time being to one of these influences, impulses, or—as the ancients called them—Signs of the Zodiac; and is demonstrating the experiencing and developing of a certain quality.

Even an entity such as a nation comes under the same law. For each nation is intended to develop, and demonstrate and be responsible for, a given quality and a certain type of genius.

It will one day be realised that this major division of the impulse of living into twelve qualities runs through all the kingdoms of nature, and that the fulfilment of nature's plan depends upon the existence, in any sphere of living, of the right proportions and expression and co-operation between these twelve qualities. Herein lies the secret of the GROUP. The evolutionary instinct causes people to come together in group formation in order to achieve objectives. Yet this constructive impulse is often short-circuited by the involutionary impulse, which causes the 'I' to produce a despotic leader in the group, which latter gives way to a lazy hero-worship. This destroys the potentiality of the expression of the twelve qualities which should exist within that group in order to make of it a perfect whole, constructively inspired.

When this secret of group formation is understood, the group will have an organic growth and form itself in the classical (atomic) pattern, with a living core which radiates. It will recognise the larger implications of group work and seek to have itself integrated as a member of a larger zodiac of groups, wherein each group was working for one of the twelve major qualities or activities. Thus the impulses towards community living amongst families, and federation between groups and finally between nations, could successfully be built upon a scientific understanding of the laws and qualities of the cosmic radiations, which in any case are playing through all of us and offering us the impulses of correct evolution.

These same cosmic laws are at work in the plant kingdom. Every species of tree, for instance, is an expression of one of the twelve Signs (or of a given planet and its minerals) and it contributes its own individual organic compound to the soil. To produce the perfect and complete soil it would be necessary to have each of the twelve Signs represented by either a tree or a plant. Therefore an understanding of this cosmic metabolism is urgently necessary in order to cure widespread soil erosion and replenish the earth according to nature's potential bounty.

The same law applies to the animal and insect world. They all have their place according to cosmic law, in order to produce a constructive and healthful symbiosis or interdependence throughout all nature. Only when this science is understood and practised can we hope to establish that radiant health and intelligent co-operation which is the much-delayed birthright of that mystery the human being. For, in the last analysis, it all depends upon him. He has the unique position, on this planet, of acting as intermediary between all the kingdoms of nature, of acting either as a destructive despot or as a *beneficent GUARDIAN*. In fact his true vocation is that of the Guardian—under God—of all His works, and of His Plan.

When one day the barriers of self-interest go down

M

between nations, and the links of understanding grow strong, they also will come together in cosmically inspired groups, and the true meaning of federation will be demonstrated. A group of nations rightly formed will bring together all the qualities of evolving human genius, thus making a perfect whole, an international atom! Several of such international atoms will eventually find themselves grouped as a major world-atom, a naturally formed world government or organisation. Then will be seen the Zodiac of Humanity, built through the love, light and power which lies waiting in the heart of every human being, every group and every nation, until the dross and debris of the past, the Dweller on the Threshold, shall have been dissolved and outgrown.

This wonderful science of living is the heritage which lies in wait for the struggling, suffering humanity of today. Many hundreds are already dimly aware of it. They are persisting with a quiet, unobtrusive heroism in their efforts to achieve the purified life in some of its aspects. It is these pioneers who could and who may bring the beginnings of a new Golden Age into being. Even the peaceful uses of atomic energy cannot alone bring to us a better life. No matter how much cheaper energy, and new spoon-fed comforts and gadgets the public is given, it will obviously continue to live in disease, disharmony and conflict, so long as it is living under the involutionary selfish impulse instead of the new and selfless one.

Only a regenerated humanity will produce a different world. Atomic energy cannot do it, any more than the discovery of fire, of the wheel, of printing, of electricity, or any other major asset did. Let us face this fact. It is of no use patiently to wait for the scientists to give us a better world with atomic energy. They will do, we may be sure, their wonderful best. But it will still be only an outer materialistic expression of a dynamic inner reality within ourselves.

In true and natural living the outer needs become less and less. A person who is radioactive, who receives inspiration with every breath he draws, has but little need of spoon-fed entertainment, of vicarious sport, and of a hundred other artificial stimulants. The present commercialised life of slavery to a vast amount of manufactured goods would give place to a world in which every person was an artisan in his own right, a creator of beauty and utility combined. This instinct and power is dammed up in every living person, as Gandhi well knew choking them, causing them blindly to seek relief in drugs, smoking, and many other doping activities.

Creative genius is not the monopoly of the intelligentsia. Throughout history the peasants of the soil have always been able to express themselves creatively in the arts and crafts, in music, singing and dancing. They have loved beauty, ceremony and ritual. They have been capable of extreme patience and devotion to the cultivation of the land and the study of nature. Such noble potentialities have largely been destroyed and submerged over and over again throughout history by the results of involutionary greed—warfare, despotism and the resulting destruction of the soil.

Finally came the greatest horror of all—the 'industrial age,' when populations have been herded into factories and condemned to a life of slavery along fixed patterns, not much better than that of the ant. The whole of humanity is still caught in the involutionary stranglehold of the profit system. It can only escape by reorienting itself to the progressive evolutionary impulse of love, of giving and sharing. This would work out in daily living as a system in which the barter of hand-made goods played a prominent part; and in which produce was grown in cosmically correct mixtures on small-holdings. These latter would be grouped in over-all planned federations, with sharing of tools and labour.

More than fifty years ago, Denmark provided successful examples of this kind of living. She turned herself into a model country, whose methods in social living, farming and folk-schools became classic.

A more recent development has been taking place since 1954 in West Bengal, which until then was a district of great poverty and low standard of living amongst the peasants. Under the influence of Vinoba, Gandhi's follower, they began, on their own initiative, to make things for each other, without the use of money. This was such a success that it developed into the Village Exchange Scheme, in which one thousand villages were active by 1955. By this means the standard of living and of culture amongst the whole population was being steadily raised. Doubtless the scheme will spread in many directions, as it later enjoyed the co-operation of the Indian Government.

In this dangerous and complex age all things are possible. It depends on whether, in the midst of the turmoil, we can with faith seek out the fundamental underlying issues, find and face the real 'facts of life', and recognise that stupendous and awe-inspiring secret which the atomic age is revealing to us.

Let us finally set down and clarify and summarise this great secret as well as we can.

In order to produce a solid material world, *love*, or the life behind manifestation, had to reverse to its negative aspect—separatism, self-centredness, possessiveness—because only those impulses create solidity and crystallisation. Thus is formed a prison in which spirit can beat out the qualities of creativeness, strength, endurance and experience. ('Without these it remains unconscious spirit, purposeless.) We can imagine that such qualities would be of use to the Creator for His purposes, and this vague assumption is about as far as our finite minds can reach. But it is a hypothesis which is upheld by a study of human nature, of history, and of the conclusions of men of genius.

The world, then, was built by the force of *love*, its negative aspect producing the involutionary descent into matter, and its positive aspect producing the evolutionary struggle to escape and return to its perfect source, plus the qualities gained in that effort.

During the descent into matter, a great proportion of all living things began to feed upon each other. The acid or positively active types were attracted to the alkaline or energy-storing types. Such 'love' in its primitive stage was expressed by grasping and devouring the thing loved. From the tiny one-cell animal devouring the tiny one-cell plant, the kingdoms of nature built themselves up on this system of inverted love. Many creatures had to take the chance of being devoured whilst still young and in the middle of their life span. Later, as the types of animals and plants became ever more advanced, nature produced many fine species of animals which did not prey upon each other, and who consumed grasses and seeds, to a degree which did not interfere with nature's economy.

Nevertheless, in the struggle for survival, and the defence against the 'devouring' principle, species over-propagated themselves until their numbers had to be kept down by other species. How much this was caused, even in the earliest times, by the interference of man when he first became agriculturist and hunter, we can only guess.

When man appeared on this planet he was by nature a frugivore, or fruit-eater. He was intended to subsist mainly upon those delicious fruits which are the *final* expression of the plant life, which are cunningly and temptingly designed to be *eaten*, in order to ensure the scattering of the seed from the parent tree. The flesh of the fruit has *finished* its life course, it is about to putrefy. There is therefore no 'devouring', no slaying, and no cutting off of a life span when fruit is consumed. It is the quintessence of the subtlest of life's metabolisms. It is the purest of all substances and the nearest to the cosmic principles, and its 'vitamins' are the product of trans-mutation itself.

This, the quintessence of all nourishment, was pro-vided by the king of the plant world, the tree, in service to the lord of the animal world, mankind! Genesis makes this quite plain. Even after man's long history of degen-eration he can still respond to a fruit diet and often is rescued by it from a condition of 'incurable disease', as we have already said.

If and when a regenerating humanity reverts little by little to its natural sustenance, the results are likely to be as follows. Firstly, it will necessitate the replanting of the planet as one great and lovely orchard. This will cure soil erosion, ensure reafforestation, and clothe the earth once more with vegetation, in such a way that rainfall and climate are resolved to their most beneficial aspects. Secondly, a humanity subsisting on a natural diet of primarily fruits and leaves would experience a revolution in mental and physical health. Its birth-rate would also fall to required moderate needs.

Thirdly, the animal kingdom, no longer preyed upon by humanity, and enjoying the benefits of the new wise husbandry, of pure soil and plentiful vegetation, would also cease from over-producing itself; and the tendency to 'devour' would largely be offset. This mysterious future development has been hinted at in the prophecy of the time when the 'lion will lie down with the lamb, and the tiger shall eat straw.'

These words bear such a powerful vibration that they are being quoted at this time in scores of humanitarian periodicals by people who feel drawn to the evolutionary love impulse which they express. The prophetic picture outlined above will be condemned as Utopian by many who have no faith in the possibility of human regeneration and its inevitable results. Yet our suggestions are, we claim, purely and scientifically practical. Man *is* a frugivore, he *is* only truly healthful that way, and *is* diseased and degenerated beyond recognition through wrong feeding. If he reverted to his true diet, it *would* produce a natural economy, with more than enough food for all, and for the animals as well. It *would* result in a lower birth-rate and healthy children. It *would* cure those conditions such as shortage of land, over-population and exploitation, which lead inevitably to war.

Therefore we claim that the picture of world regeneration which we have outlined is essentially a natural and practical one. However, it can, of course, only be achieved by degrees. No fanatical and over-hasty efforts are to be recommended. They would bring unfortunate results in their train and would damage the prospects of a New Age. We must first gradually accustom ourselves to the possibility of a new way of living. We must yearn after our own soul or supraconscious, until we finally begin to make contact. We should remember that our own core of latent love or atomic energy is there within us, and is the only gateway to a future heaven on earth. As we were told, Heaven lies within us!

Surely if we are prepared to give a certain number of hours to sleeping, eating, earning our living and entertaining ourselves, we should allocate a reasonable amount of time to the greatest occupation of all—that of coming really *alive* and aware of the world of reality, of our nature and purpose, and of the way of achieving our glorious heritage?

Let us, little by little, reach for our inner consciousness, our 'still small voice', until it begins to be with us all the time, and every cell in our minds and bodies is stimulated towards a magic transmutation. Let us take true pride in having been born as a potential 'Son of God' and a Guardian of this planet. Let us move with courage towards our 'Second Birth' into the new awareness of *responsibility*. Let us begin, little by little, to study what God intended this world to become, and the ways in which He planned evolution through symbiosis and radioactivity. Let us face up to our 'sins of omission', where we have failed to co-operate or to understand.

This will mean that we gradually will wish to cease from using those products which reach us at the cost of suffering, drudgery, wrong living and exploitation, in any of the kingdoms of nature.

We will not wish to be accessaries to the extravagant use of the land, to the cause of soil erosion, to the pollution of air, water or earth with unnatural chemicals, to the exploitation of our fellow-beings, anywhere causing them to perform work which degrades them spiritually, or injures their physical health; to the enslavement of the animal kingdom in a hundred ways; and to the denuding of the planet of its natural tree covering.

In this light the first things which will stand condemned will be flesh-eating, the use of tobacco, alcohol, tea and coffee and other extravagant consumers of the land and destroyers of health. Next we will look askance at much of the mining and industrial labour, in particular that which brings about disease, smog, or stultifying mechanical drudgery. We will not wish to be a party to the profit system. We will be against the ridiculous practice of resorting to violence, or the threat of violence, in the cause of peace! Above all, we will not wish to be a party to hypocrisy, and will face squarely up to those injunctions which are fundamental to all the great spiritual religions, such as the practice of love and harmlessness towards friend and 'enemy' alike. Finally, we will see it as our privilege and duty to study natural law as it is found in all the kingdoms of nature, and to mould our lives in alignment with it.

If and when we have achieved this reorientation of our viewpoint on life, and of our sense of values, we will begin to know what we, as adult human beings, *require* the producers of atomic energy to do for us all. Is it to be ever more spoon-fed entertainment, more millions spent on wars and armaments, and on the hopeless fight against disease caused by wrong living?

Or are we, as determined awakened adult persons, going to demand the right to play our parts in deciding on new ways of living; on shorter hours of drudgery; on the development of the human being *himself*, with all his wonderful potentialities; on the study and practice of personal transmutation; on reconciliation with the animal kingdom and its emancipation; on the cleansing of the planet of poisons in air, water and earth; on the intelligent replanting of the earth along scientifically natural lines; on the study of the ideal communal co-operative way of life, freed from the profit system; on the personal governing of firstly the self, and secondly the environment, as a basis for eventual federation and a world government wherein we each play our part.

All these projects will be thrilling, exhilarating and fascinating ones to work out. They will bring peoples together all over the world in a bond of that warm and deep friendship which exists where no self-interest is, and where all are obeying the spiritual impulse from within, which is identical in every human heart. So much of this is happening already that we no longer merit the accusation of Utopianism! We can point in all directions to the emerging of the new humanity.

We can see traces of the new humanity amongst the scientists themselves. Soon we will be able no longer to speak of science, rightly or wrongly as materialistic. For instance, this is what the American scientist, David Dietz, who worked so closely with the development of the Atom Bomb, says in his book *Atomic Energy*: 'If science brought only its practical applications, it might indeed prove the eventual undoing of mankind. But science brings also a spirit, its own guiding spirit, and in this there is hope for mankind. To the scientist the practical applications have always been secondary. He has sought primarily to understand nature and the universe. Galileo, meditating upon the laws of motion, was trying to understand the workings of nature. So was Einstein when he wrote the equation for the release of atomic energy, and Rutherford when he began his atom-smashing experiments. This does not mean that science is contemptuous of its practical uses. The opposite is true. But it does mean that the true scientist is motivated by a higher aim than that of making life easier. He wishes also to ennoble and to enrich life.'

If there are in fact, amongst the most brilliant of the atomic scientists of today, men of noble spiritual impulse, it will be enthralling to wait for their conclusions when they reach the last intimate stages of discovery within the core of the atom. As we have said, the thing which is waiting for them there is nothing less than that magic and mysterious force—the love of God for that which

He has made and is holding together. How long will it be before this dawns upon the scientists?

Their present stage is well described by David Dietz, who writes: 'The fact of the matter is that we are very much puzzled by the forces which hold the nucleus of the atom together. The outer structure of the atom is easily understood. The combined negative electric charge of the outer electrons equals the positive charge supplied by the protons in the nucleus. But from a consideration of electric forces the nucleus ought not even to exist, for it is a closely packed combination of positive and neutral particles. The positive particles ought to repel each other with the utmost violence, causing the nucleus to fly apart. Such repulsion between positively charged particles is a well-known fact. It is apparent, therefore, that some force comes into action in the minute distances within the nucleus of the atom. We have spoken of this as the binding force, but giving it a name is no explanation of what it is.'

If the day should come when the scientists do discover what *it* is—that the ultimate force within the atom with which they have to deal is the love of God—what significance will that have for them? Faced with such an awe-inspiring 'scientific fact', what will they do about it? What, in fact, could they do about it? How much do we already know about this force?

Surely this is the force which, when radiated by a human being, can heal, can rejuvenate and can renew? It can do this on the physical plane, revivifying the bodies of plants and animals, and of fellow-human beings. It can do this on the psychical levels, bringing about transmutations, realisations, illuminations and mental healing. Christ used this force and taught the use of it.

The Alchemists sought to *capture* this volatile force by

gentle and subtle methods, purifying and transmuting the body in which it dwelt without allowing the force to escape.

Modern scientists, on the contrary, produce radio-activity by such violent means that the love-force is hurled out of the outraged atom, and lost for ever. Only its lower physical counterpart, 'atomic energy', remains.

Yet, could the scientists find a means of reverently and gently retaining that love-force so that it could be drawn upon, what unimaginable possibilities might then be available for the aid of humanity! All other methods of healing would become obsolete. Religion and science would have become one, and would be dealing not with hypotheses but with reality. The cleansing force of atomic-love-energy would do much to melt the 'Dweller on the Threshold', the crystallised thought-habits which prevent man from achieving that finer development of his senses which will reveal the inner worlds to him. It would help him to escape from the mental disease of separateness, and on its radiations he could unite in understanding with the rest of the living world.

Therefore it would be of the greatest aid in the emergence of the new spirit of Guardianship which is struggling to be born. It is of vital interest to all those who long to work for world regeneration. Atomic-love-energy, whether wielded by the coming Guardians of the New Age through their own personal vibrations, or whether captured in its simpler form by the future atomic scientists, will be the great new epoch-making factor which will help to bring in a Golden Age such as we cannot dream of at this day. But it will only be achieved through renunciation of more crude and violent methods, and of more worldly gains—there will have to be that choice!

Let it not be thought that the possibilities we have here envisaged are too fantastic or unlikely. Let us, on the contrary, make haste to study them, unless we wish to be left far behind. Already the trail has been well blazed. Let me quote from a 'World Goodwill Bulletin' recently published: 'It is therefore most encouraging and significant to learn of a centre whose entire resources are devoted to the systematic and scientific study of the higher energies and powers of man, and in particular the nature, functioning and power of creative altruism or love. Such a centre is the Harvard University Research Centre in Creative Altruism in the United States, founded in 1949. One of the two main assumptions on which the work of the Harvard Research Centre is based is that "unselfish creative love" is a tremendous power for good, and that if men knew how to release and direct this energy, it would render great service to humanity. Professor Sorokin, who founded and directs the Centre, draws an analogy between *the potential energy stored in the human heart and the energy stored in the atom.* The release of this energy in a sufficient number of people could have far-reaching effects. We know little as yet about man's higher and creative powers, but the concept of love as an energy and power is much more fundamental than the idea that it is desire or sentiment. The second main assumption made by the Research Centre is that the problems of our age and civilisation can only be solved by a significant increase in the altruistic transformation of "persons, groups, institutions and culture".'

Thus we can see today the beautiful spirit of guardianship coming alive in people of every race—black, white, yellow and brown. They are stretching out their hands to each other across the world in a fellowship whose power will finally cleanse humanity from the obscene evils of war and exploitation. Thus, through individual human regeneration, will the real 'atomic age' be brought in, that Golden Age prophesied so firmly by the esoteric writings of the Ageless Wisdom.

Let us conclude our search, therefore, with a few quotations from one of the most profound of modern books on the Ageless Wisdom, that of *Cosmic Fire* by Alice Bailey. This book was, by 1925, dictated to her by a living Tibetan sage, who would seem to be an example of what we have described as a transmuted and perfected human genius. Here is a paragraph from the book, dealing with the atomic structure which informs the whole universe:

'In all these atoms, stupendous or minute, microcosmic or macrocosmic, the central life corresponds to the positive charge of electrical force predicted by science, whether it is the life of a cosmic Entity such as a solar Logos, or the tiny elemental life within a physical atom. The lesser atoms which revolve round their positive centre, and which are at present termed electrons by science, are the negative aspect, and this is true not only of the atom on the physical plane, but of the human atoms, held to their central attractive point, a Heavenly Man, or the atomic forms which in their aggregate form the recognised solar system. All forms are built up in an analogous manner and the only difference consists—as the text-books teach—in the arrangement and number of the electrons. The electron itself will eventually be found to be an elemental tiny life.'

Regarding transmutation, it said: 'Transmutation is the passage across from one state of being to another through the agency of fire' . . . 'The religious man, especially the Christian, recognises the psychic quality of this transmutative power, and frequently speaks in the sacred books, of the soul being tried or tested seven times in the fire' . . . and again, 'Radiation is transmutation in process of accomplishment.'

It is also promised that: 'The time will come, when the attitude of man to the animal kingdom will be revolutionised, and the slaughter, ill-treatment, and that form of cruelty called "sport", will be done away with.' Speaking of medical progress: 'It will come when the medical profession concentrates upon preventive action, substituting sunshine, a vegetarian diet, and the application of the laws of magnetic vibration and vitality for the present regimen of drugs and surgical operations. Then will come the time when finer and better human beings will manifest on earth.'

After speaking of the vast and mysterious powers which have man under their influence, there follows this paragraph:

'Nevertheless, within limits, man definitely does "control his destiny", and can initiate action which produces effects recognisable by him as being dependent upon his activity along a particular line. He does, on a miniature scale, repeat the procedure of the Logos on a vaster scale, and thus is the arbiter of his own destiny, the producer of his own drama, the architect of his own home, and the initiator of his own affairs. Though he may be the meeting place of forces outside his control, yet he can utilise force, circumstance and environment and can turn them, if he so will, to his own ends.'

Thus we may glimpse a long vista of wonder and of achievement lying ahead for us all. Let us go forward with courage and inspiration, grasping our new privilege of responsibility. Let us step through the gateway of selflessness to the unknown freedom and unimaginable power of the transmuted, of true adulthood, and of the 'Second Birth'.

Bibliography

The Secret Doctrine, by H. P. Blavatsky.
The Rosicrucian Cosmo-Conception, by Max Heindel.
The Secret of Life, by Georges Lakhovsky. (Heinemann.)
Cosmic Fire, by Alice Bailey. (Lucis Trust.)
Principles of Light and Colour, by Dr. Babbitt.
The Initiation of the World, by Vera Stanley Alder. (Rider.)
Modern Alchemy, by Dorothy Fisk. (Faber.)
Atomic Energy, by David Dietz. (Westhouse.)
Krishnamurti Writings, Inc., London.
World Goodwill Information and Research Service.
The Millennium Guild, New York.

The author would be glad to hear from readers who are interested in the subject of world guardianship.